CU00943307

Forty years before 'mad cow disease' a similar c~
and Westminster. The tobacco industry - funda
provided 14% of tax revenue) and hitherto of un.........-------- , .
was suspected of killing its customers. But it took half a generation to move
from scientific proof to effective government action as a cohort of purblind
politicians and officials made place for their less blinkered successors.

Expert statements from advisory groups and the Medical Research Council
were watered down and ignored. Iain Macleod chain-smoked while he
made the first Ministry of Health announcement on the subject. The
Treasury lost no opportunity to protect the source of so much revenue.

Meantime the industry bought favour - and confusion - with a gift of
£250,000 to fund research and lobbied assiduously with their disingenuous
reinterpretation of the statistics. The way top tobacco company managers
casually visited Permanent Secretaries to press their points bears careful
reading by anyone concerned today about government departments that fail
to keep a critical distance from powerful industries pressing their
commercial interests.

'This book records,' says **Sir George Godber** in his Foreword, 'how proven
facts can be obscured by commercial interests.' The first Chief Medical
Officer to take the problem seriously, he says that as a result 'the message
reaching much of the public remains unclear.'

' . . . as absorbing to read as a good detective novel. It is, however, much
more. Its publication should help avoid any similar delay in the future when
medical research has revealed how tens - or, as we now know, hundreds - of
thousands of premature deaths can be avoided in this country alone every
year' - from the Foreword by **Sir Richard Doll**.

David Pollock *was Director of Action on Smoking and Health from 1991 to 1994
and remains a member of the ASH Advisory Council.*

Denial
&
Delay

David Pollock

*(sometime Director of
Action on Smoking and Health)*

Denial
& Delay

The Political History of
Smoking and Health, 1951-1964:
Scientists, Government and Industry
as seen in the papers at the
Public Records Office

Forewords by
Sir Richard Doll
and
Sir George Godber

Action on Smoking and Health

Set in Garamond in WordPerfect 6.1

Printed by Juma, Sheffield

Copyright © David Pollock, 1999

The moral right of the author has been asserted..

ISBN 1 872428 44 4

Published by
Action on Smoking and Health
102-108 Clifton Street
London EC2A 4HW

Contents

Foreword

by Sir Richard Doll CH FRS FRCP

In retrospect, it is now clear that evidence of the harmful effects on health of smoking tobacco had been accumulating for some hundred years before 1950, but until then it had made little impact on the medical profession and none at all on the general public. In Britain, the increase in the mortality from lung cancer had attracted the attention of pathologists in the 1920s, but it was not until after the second world war that the increase had become so pronounced that intensive efforts were made to find an explanation for it. Then, in 1950, five reports were published linking the risk of the disease to the individual's smoking habits, which led to the conclusion that smoking was an important cause of the disease. By that time, however, smoking had become such a normal habit - 85 per cent of middle aged men being regular smokers - that people found it hard to believe that it could be an important cause of disease and even the massive data contained in these five papers continued to be almost totally ignored, as had been the less detailed data in the three other similar papers that had been published in the previous decade.

Not everyone, however, ignored them. Dr Horace Joules, in particular, Medical Director of the Central Middlesex Hospital and a distinguished physician, was determined that the Ministry should do something about them. Moreover, he was in a position to see that they did, for he was a member of both the Ministry's Central Health Service Council and its Standing Advisory Committee on Cancer and Radiotherapy, and the action he proposed started a series of events at government level that it would be hard to believe was not conceived by a satirical novelist, if they had not been documented in official reports, memoranda, and committee minutes which have been released for public examination 30 years after they were written.

The result of David Pollock's research into these official documents provides a detailed account of how, at first advisory committees, then health ministry staff, and finally cabinet ministers themselves were able to prevaricate and postpone any decisive action to discourage smoking for 13 years after Dr Joules had proposed that the Ministry should undertake a publicity campaign about its dangers. The tobacco industry, not surprisingly, played a major role in delaying action, but it would not have had so much success had it not been aided first by the hesitation of some of the Ministry's scientific advisers to accept the validity of findings that had not been made by standard procedures of laboratory research and later by the economic interests of the Treasury and the Board of Trade.

The account of how these various interests influenced political action provides a notable example of the way in which government policies are determined in a market economy. It will, I suspect, find its way into many political textbooks. Meanwhile it is as absorbing to read as a good detective novel. It is, however, much more. For its publication should help to avoid any similar delay in the future, when medical research has revealed ways in which tens - or, as we now know, hundreds - of thousands of premature deaths can be avoided in this country alone every year.

Richard Doll

Oxford
July 1999

Foreword

by Sir George Godber FRCOG FRCPsych

Almost half a century ago we learned that smoking was the main cause of lung cancer. Albeit our knowledge in 1950 was so limited, it would have led to real action at once had it not been for opposition for commercial and political reasons - the latter due to the substantial tax revenue from tobacco.

An emphatic reduction in smoking in the mid-1950s could have prevented millions of premature deaths by now. I calculated for an annual report as Chief Medical Officer thirty years ago that eliminating smoking would preserve 180,000 years of working life each year. By today's knowledge that must be a vast underestimate.

One must not, of course, judge the authorities of the 1950s by the standards of today. We were not attuned then to the idea of preventive change that would yield assessable benefit in twenty or more years. Our experience was rather in such action as diphtheria immunisation with 50,000 cases and 2,000 deaths preventable each year in the short term. Yet one can only look back with a feeling of guilt at doing so little.

What this book makes plain, however, is that the Government knew at least a large part of the harm smoking did but needed the tax revenue so much that it did not want prevention to succeed. Iain Macleod was a good Minister and my friend - but how could one now accept a health minister who faces a press conference on the strong reasons for refraining from smoking - and smokes while he does it?

But politicians are not alone in this. It was disturbing for me to learn from this book of the close relations in the 1950s between the tobacco industry and some of my senior colleagues in the Ministry of Health. But even in the late 1960s when members of the Medical Research Council were photographed at their 50th anniversary meeting, I had to point out that there was an ash tray between each pair of members at the table: they were hastily removed! The Royal College of Physicians went on allowing smoking at its meetings and occasions for over twenty years after the report of 1962. I had persuaded the Ministry's Standing Medical Advisory Council and Central Health Services Council to ban it long before that - and WHO to remove smoking impedimenta from their meetings..

In the years that followed we have discovered that even more premature deaths from many other conditions are also due to smoking. Yet the commercially oriented opposition has steadily mounted and the message reaching much of the public remains unclear. Still today far too many people smoke.

This book records how proven facts can be obscured by commercial interests and even more how a habit linked to an addictive drug can lead to the disregard of danger. We need to learn the lessons it offers.

George Godber

Cambridge
July 1999

Preface

This is a study of how politicians, officials and the tobacco industry handled the crisis when the link between smoking and lung cancer was established. It is based almost exclusively on official records at the Public Records Office at Kew.

During my last year with Action on Smoking and Health (1995) I had the privilege of being employed to do writing and research for them, and *inter alia* I chose to study as fully as possible the records on tobacco at Kew. ASH has my complete transcripts and photocopies and an index of files with descriptive notes on their content. Happily the files were then already open up to 1964 and therefore covered the whole period to the change of government that year, which forms a natural terminus to my story. I have, however, recently returned to Kew to consult a few more recent files to tie up loose ends.

I am clear that I have not traced all the relevant files. I found nothing from the Home Office or the Ministry of Education except stray papers on other departments' files. I have not been to Edinburgh to inspect the files of the Scottish Office Health Department, which was notably more enlightened than its Whitehall cousin. However, the Medical Research Council, Ministry of Health, Board of Trade and Cabinet Office files on which I have principally relied certainly tell the main story.

I am particularly grateful to Professor Sir Richard Doll and Sir George Godber, not only for providing forewords but also for reading my study in draft and providing valuable comments, which I have incorporated. I am in Sir Richard's debt also for his encouragement to complete the work when other preoccupations pushed it aside for many months.

I should like finally to commend the helpfulness of the staff at Kew, despite frustrations with their indexes which, however compendious, still sometimes confront one with impenetrable portmanteau titles such as 'Papers: 1960-61'.

My work has a narrow focus but tells a story not previously related. As the tobacco industry's long history of deceit and cover-up, fully established now by documents from its own files, leads to pressure for more stringent legislation, I hope it may be salutary to have on record the prevarication and procrastination of a past generation of civil servants and politicians to make us all a little sceptical about any suggestion that cases are not yet made or that proposals are unworkable or too radical.

The lessons are perhaps being learned in this country, but 'big tobacco' rules rampant throughout much of the third world. Truly radical moves are needed to control an industry that makes immense profits by killing a customer every ten seconds year in, year out - and within 20 or 30 years from now will unashamedly have tripled that rate of killing. Perhaps the most encouraging development of the last few years is the serious discussion of an international treaty to control this cancer feeding on human society.

David Pollock

Stoke Newington
July 1999

Notes and Sources

The notes at chapter ends include the sources for the material to which they refer. Comprehensive Public Records Office (PRO) file references are given to enable future investigators to follow up my points. Many papers, of course, appear on more than one file: generally only a single reference is given here.

PRO file prefixes signify the department owning the file as follows:

BT: Board of Trade

CAB: Cabinet Office, including the office of the Lord President of the Council

FD: Medical Research Council

MH: Ministry of Health

T: Treasury

Prologue

In January 1935, Sir Gilbert Barling, chairman of the Birmingham branch of the British Empire Cancer Campaign (now the Cancer Research Campaign), having secured £1,000 for the purpose, wrote to the Medical Research Council asking who, so endowed, might investigate 'the asserted marked increase in cancer of the lung' by looking into the statistics, both in the UK and abroad, conducting experimental work on atmospheric deposits, examining the effects of traffic, surgery, better diagnosis and other relevant factors. Professor Sir Edward Mellanby, Secretary of the MRC, replied that £1,000 was surely too little for so wide a survey - and the survey too wide for any one person. Sir Gilbert's discouraged response, the last item on this thin file at the Public Record Office, dwells on his own age and infirmity, and the project seems to have been dropped.[1]

Nearly seven years later, a letter reached the MRC from a Wallasey general practitioner, Lennox Johnston, who had 'for about twelve years . . . been engaged on an investigation into the effects of smoking on health . . . This work has cost me over £10,000 and nearly my life with nicotine' (which he had experimented with, injecting himself and others with up to 1/8th grain) . With the nation at war and in the conviction that his findings were of importance to the war effort, he had prepared a script for a broadcast talk, but the BBC had rejected it. Not, as the file repeatedly reveals, his own best advocate, Johnston had written of smoking as an addiction protected by a taboo analogous to that preventing discussion of sex and had pointed out that, while 'Adolf Hitler neither smokes nor drinks', Winston Churchill's 'cigar represents, I suggest, a symbol for our nation. It is a symbol of luxury and drugs'. If the nation quit smoking and drinking, he foresaw a 'gigantic National renaissance' leading to 'increased factory output and . . . increased fighting efficiency': 'by conquering our weakness we should become unconquerable'.

The thesis he put to the MRC, however, was percipient. Smokers smoked for the effect of the nicotine, but their health suffered through the effect of the smoke on their lungs. Men smoked ten times as much as women, and their death rates after the age of 40 from 'practically all the respiratory diseases, including phthisis and respiratory cancer, were more than double the female . . . There is no doubt that this drug [*viz.* nicotine] could be administered by a means less damaging to the respiratory system and unpleasant to non-smokers and yet with equal satisfaction to smokers, e.g., by atomizer, losenge etc.'

He sought support for a comparative study of time lost at work by matched groups of smokers and non-smokers. Apparently ignored by the MRC (despite two follow-up letters, one not for the last time denying that he was a crank), he wrote again in October 1942 proposing comparative studies of smokers and non-smokers in the Army and saying that the Director-General, Army Medical Services had agreed to cooperate if the MRC approved. He added, doubtless not helping his case, that he had had a paper on 'Tobacco Smoking and Respiratory Disease' rejected by the editor of the *British Medical Journal* which he 'resented because the editor of the B.M.J. is a cigarette inhaler and one of the most important points in my paper is that on issues relating to this drug, the judgment of the addict is unconsciously disturbed.'

The MRC, in the person of Dr Arthur Landsborough Thomson, its Principal Assistant Secretary, sought an explanation of the Army's backing from the Director of Medical Research at the War Office, Brigadier F A E Crew, commenting: 'I may say frankly that we are not impressed by Dr Johnston's proposals'. Brig. Crew replied: 'A.M.D. [Army Medical Department] would be glad to cooperate if the M.R.C. approves the investigation. I should be very surprised indeed to learn, however, that such approval is given.' It was apparently their policy always to agree to proposed enquiries in principle and leave others - like the MRC - to turn them down. This, after a meeting in January 1943 with Mellanby at which Johnston became excited and angry, they duly did; and despite several self-exculpatory letters from him, thereafter he received nothing but formal replies until 1948, by which time his renewed proposals were rejected since they had (he was told in confidence) been overtaken by work the MRC had commissioned from Professor Austin Bradford Hill and Dr Richard Doll. In this letter of rejection, Dr F H K Green, the MRC assistant secretary, wrote that there was already plenty of evidence of the deleterious effects of smoking and added prophetically 'Even if it were possible to prove a correlation between smoking and coronary thrombosis - or, in your own investigation, smoking and cancer of the lung - I do not think the smoking public would pay much heed to it'. Johnston replied (*ad hominem* as always) that he inferred from this comment that Green was a smoker, to which Green replied lamely: 'I hardly smoke at all'.

Johnston had a short piece published in *The Lancet*[2], picked a quarrel with Bradford Hill, falsely accusing him of keeping him off a television programme[3] on smoking in January 1953, obtained application forms for a research grant from the MRC in August that year, but then disappears from the record.[4]

When Johnston was told in October 1948 of the work by Austin Bradford Hill and Richard Doll it was already almost two-and-a-half years since the first moves that led to that momentous collaboration. In May 1946 R J R Farrow, Deputy Registrar-General, wrote to J E Pater, an assistant secretary at the Ministry of Health, about moves within the British Empire Cancer Campaign to set up an investigation of cancer of the lung. These originated with Dr Percy Stocks, who was Chief Medical Statistician at the General Register Office from 1933 to 1950 but in this instance seems to have been working through the BECC group in Chester and North Wales. He had won the backing of Malcolm Donaldson, chairman of the statistical committee of the Radium Commission. Farrow wrote: 'In the view of Stocks the continual increase in deaths attributed to cancer of the lung, about 8% every year, is a serious matter which ought to be studied with a view to deciding the vexed question whether it can really be attributed to more X-ray examinations, which is the facile explanation, or, if not, what is causing it.' He suggested that an investigation sponsored by the MRC or the Minister's Medical Advisory Committee would be preferable to one by 'a more or less private committee' as proposed.

The Ministry took the views of Sir Ernest Rock Carling, its highly distinguished adviser on all matters related to cancer and radiotherapy[5], and Lord Amulree, one of its medical officers, and then asked the MRC to take on the work. In June, Sir Edward Mellanby wrote 'I am in favour of a statistical investigation . . . Would it not be possible for Stocks to get in touch with Bradford Hill and arrange for an investigation of this kind to be made by the Statistical Committee of the Medical Research Council? It might be interesting to know not only the relative incidence of cancer of the lung in different trades, but also whether there is any difference between town and country dwellers, and whether smoking, especially cigarette smoking, is of any importance, etc. . .', although, as Dr Green of the MRC wrote to Bradford Hill two weeks later, 'Mellanby . . . is doubtful whether the information obtained would throw much light on the question of aetiology.' Agreeing to Green's suggestion of a conference, Bradford Hill pointed out: 'The much greater rise in the death rate of men compared with women suggests that X-ray examinations are not the sole answer though no doubt contributory.'

The informal MRC conference on the lung cancer problem was held on 6 February 1947. Among the thirteen people present were Stocks (who took the chair), Amulree, Rock Carling, Donaldson, Bradford Hill, Mellanby,

Professor Alexander Haddow and Professor and Mrs E L Kennaway. In a ten-page brief for the meeting, Stocks wrote of the increase in lung cancer being greater in towns than rural areas, greater in the north than the south, and greater in areas of less rather than more sunshine. 'The only adequate explanations of these facts which can be suggested are that either smokiness or pollution of the atmosphere in certain towns is an important causative factor for lung cancer or else that sunshine is an important preventive factor. The former explanation receives support from the finding that occupations connected with coal gas production, certain dusty trades and tobacco, have lung cancer mortalities above the average.' A table showing no correlation between tobacco consumption and incidence of lung cancer in a number of countries was annotated that the data were not reliable.

Professor Kennaway observed that 'the absence of class differences in lung cancer rates suggested that the environmental causative factor was to be found in the atmosphere or in some other influence to which all sections of the population were subject', adding (ignoring the problem of delayed reaction that was so often to confuse the question) that if coal smoke pollution, which had been on the decrease, were postulated, the increase in incidence of lung cancer could not be explained. He 'thought it unlikely that sunlight had a direct protective action' as coal miners had low rates of lung cancer, although sunlight might 'act indirectly by destroying a carcinogenic substance - e.g., benzpyrene - in the atmosphere' but he 'suggested that smoking, particularly of cigarettes, might be responsible'.[6]

Other theories put forward included arsenic in cigarette smoke, radioactive dusts, and drugs. The outcome of the conference was that Professors Haddow and Kennaway should continue to investigate benzpyrene in cigarette smoke and arsenic, radioactivity and benzpyrene in atmospheric pollution samples collected by the Department of Scientific and Industrial Research, while a further meeting would be held to plan 'a large scale statistical study of the past smoking habits of those with cancer of the lung, and of two control groups, one consisting of patients with cancer of the stomach and the other of diabetics.'

The conference minute adds that 'Sir Edward Mellanby said that the Council would probably be prepared to pay the salary of a whole-time worker for this study.'[7] By summer, however, Mellanby was suggesting that, partly for reasons of economy, the work should be assigned to the MRC's new Social Medicine Research Unit rather than to Bradford Hill's statistical unit. Hill replied vigorously rejecting the suggestion and writing of his and Stocks' being 'intensely interested' and of there being no economies by doing the work elsewhere. As to 'medical supervision . . . I shall have a Rockefeller Scholar in my department who might be used on it at little cost. A much better alternative would be Richard Doll who has been employed by the Council in the survey of peptic ulcer *(sic)* in industry and which is coming to an end I believe. I do know he is interested in cancer of the lung and I regard him as a very good worker to whom it is well worth while giving a wider experience in medical statistical work with an eye to the future. As you know, the number of medical persons who take at all kindly to careful statistical work is still small . . .'

Mellanby gave grudging consent to the Statistical Unit doing the work: 'It seems to me that one of the main reasons against your Department carrying out the work is the extra medical cost involved, but if you can get your Rockefeller scholar to do this, that point is no longer worth consideration.'[8] Bradford Hill had won his main point and played for time on the question of a medical appointment.

Bradford Hill, Kennaway[9] and Stocks now prepared a draft protocol[10] for the planned retrospective investigation. This opened by identifying 'the main problem at issue' as the 'possible association' between lung cancer and tobacco smoking but said 'it would clearly be unwise to limit attention entirely to smoking'. It proposed administering a questionnaire to lung cancer patients notified by cooperating hospitals. To ensure uniformity and completeness questionnaires would need to be filled in by specially appointed 'well qualified social workers' who would interview the patients, and to save travel costs the Greater London area was proposed. Control groups of patients with stomach cancer and patients with diseases other than cancer would be included in the study - the latter being picked by the social workers to match their lung cancer patients for sex and 'approximately, if possible, . . . age - subject, of course to the patient being in a fit state to be interviewed'. Estimates on the basis of 1942 statistics (the latest available) suggested that two staff would be sufficient, each conducting seven 30-minute interviews per day.

The draft questionnaire sought not only a medical history and detailed history of the patients' smoking but also their occupational history and places of residence since birth, together with the forms of heating in the workroom and living room respectively and the proximity of the nearest gas works to their homes. There were questions also about how often before the war they ate fried fish 'cooked at home' or 'from shop', or 'fried bacon, sausage, ham, cooked at home', and 'Women patients only: fat generally used for frying pre-war'.

These proposals were discussed at a second MRC conference[11] on 29 September 1947 where Bradford Hill took the chair and the Ministry of Health was represented (but Amulree, Rock Carling, Haddow and Stocks were absent). The conference suggested extending the control group to include patients with cancer of the colon and rectum as well as the stomach and duodenum 'to prevent any bias due to products of tobacco being swallowed with the saliva' and made other proposals, including extra questions ('the amount of time spent out of doors during work and leisure' is annotated in manuscript 'Impossible').

They also, doubtless at Bradford Hill's instigation, recorded their view that 'the investigation would necessitate at least part-time direction by a medical man', and formally recommended the proposals to the MRC.

At this stage Bradford Hill wrote to Dr Martin Ware, the MRC administrative officer, suggesting that Richard Doll be shown the previous papers so that he could comment on the paper to be put to the Council with the final proposal: 'I have already talked to him tentatively and I know he is interested. If we are going to put his name forward as a whole or part time worker on it we ought to know what he thinks.' Ware agreed, and the formal paper[12] to the Council on the study included 'the appointment from January 1st, 1948 and, in the first place, for one year of W R S Doll, MD MRCP, to organise and direct the investigation at a part-time salary of £600 per annum', along with two full-time social workers at £350 each to interview the patients, and a grant towards expenses of £300 per annum.

The study now commenced. It was not happening in a vacuum. The economy was struggling: the winter of 1947 had been one of the bitterest on record, rationing was becoming tighter, and dollar imports - such as 88% of the tobacco consumed in Britain - were tightly restricted. The April 1947 budget increased the price of cigarettes by a shilling - about 40-45% - leading to protests in Parliament about the hardship caused to pensioners. A Treasury official recorded the next day: 'The Chancellor [Hugh Dalton] has been thinking over the question of a possible concession on tobacco to old age pensioners in the light of yesterday's debate, and he has come to the pretty firm conclusion that a special arrangement of some kind must be devised . . .' After much debate tokens worth 2s 0d a week (10 cigarettes cost about 1s 8d at the time) were issued to pensioners who declared themselves to be habitual users of tobacco or snuff[13] - a concession terminated only in 1958[14].

All purchases of US tobacco were stopped on 22 October. In December 1947, Sir Edward Bridges, Permanent Secretary at the Treasury, wrote to Sir John Woods, his opposite number at the Board of Trade: 'The Chancellor [Sir Stafford Cripps] has given instructions that we should consider what action should be taken in the April Budget in the light of the probability that we shall not be able to afford any purchases of tobacco at all next year.' Woods' reply included a manuscript postscript: 'The probability that we shall not be able to afford tobacco is one thing . . . the probability of our having to take dollar tobacco on a Marshall [Aid] string is another!' (The point was borne out by a later minute: 'The UK is the only really important market for the Virginia type of tobacco that we smoke and the speed with which the American Government stepped in to purchase the 1948 crop once we had withdrawn from the market is an indication of their nervousness about the internal effects of a cessation of British demand.')

A working party began considering the alternatives of rationing or 'a further steep increase in the tobacco duty'. Its report in January 1948, marked Top Secret, concluded that rationing would be impractical as it would lead to a black market in coupons as non-smokers and light smokers sold to heavy smokers, with the risk of undermining the rationing of food which was already needing stricter enforcement because of the 'weakening of the public conscience' in the face of the general decrease in food supplies. A joint ration for tobacco and sweets would reduce the black market because non-smokers would use the ration for sweets, but sweet coupons could be used for tobacco, substituting adults' tobacco for children's sweets, which was undesirable as 'Ministry of Food experts attach importance to the nutritional value of sweets'; and a joint ration would create difficulties with retailers.

The report remarks: 'As to the number of non-smokers, the only recent estimates we have seen suggest that one-fifth of the men and one-half of the women do not smoke at all. These figures appear to be somewhat on the high side and we have assumed that 15% of the men and 40% of the women do not smoke.'

It adds: 'We ought also to call attention to a possible long-term effect on the revenue of either rationing or a heavy increase of duty. It is probable that many people will permanently adopt the lower level of consumption enforced by rationing or an increase of duty and that others will be induced by a heavy increase of duty to give up smoking altogether. Such results would mean a permanent, and in the long run substantial, loss of revenue at any given level of duty.' This worry about the revenue effects of reduced smoking recurs throughout the years.

The working party ended with a tentative recommendation of another 50% increase in tax: the increase in 1947 had produced a reduction in demand variously estimated at the time as 12-15% or 20% but put at 17% in a 1964 review; a further 50% increase (lifting the price of 20 Gold Flake from 3s 4d to 4s 8d) would perhaps cut consumption by about a third with neutral effect to the Revenue. In the event the tax increase in 1948 was restricted to 2d.[15]

None of Whitehall's concern was known to the public, of course, nor to the MRC's investigators - nor, of course, could the Treasury know of the eventual outcome of Bradford Hill and Doll's study, though whether they would have linked such knowledge with worries about the dollar crisis to adopt policies based on public health must be strongly doubted.

In January 1948, the MRC wrote to a number of London hospitals seeking their cooperation in the planned study by notifying Dr Doll of all patients diagnosed with cancer of the lung, bronchus, stomach, rectum and colon and by allowing the social workers to interview these patients and a randomly chosen control group with non-cancer diseases. By 1 May 1948 Doll was reporting on the first 156 interviews, saying there was already some bias towards smoking in lung cancer patients - but also towards residence near gasworks (or maybe, he noted, merely gasholders: not everyone would know the difference; and anyway the link disappeared as the study continued). A third social worker was engaged by June and in September Doll's ten-page interim report stated: 'The results appear to show a definite association between carcinoma of the lung and smoking, an association which is less strong for pipe smokers than for cigarette smokers', although the lack of correlation between inhaling and cancer was 'surprising'. No correlation was evident for the other cancers. By today's standards the most interesting aspect of the statistics is the extent of smoking among the control patients: of 143 men with lung cancer, all smoked, but so did 135 of the 143 controls.[16]

In October the extension of the one-year study through 1949 was agreed, and in a lengthy fourth interim report in September 1949 Doll concluded 'It is, therefore, probable that there is a real association between ca. lung and smoking.' Less guardedly the same month he wrote to Dr Green at the MRC: 'Incidentally the investigation has gone much better than I expected and it looks as if smoking will be incriminated to a major extent!'[17]

The following month, Green recorded a meeting between himself, Doll and Dr Harold Himsworth, the new Secretary of the MRC: 'After challenging Doll on a number of detailed points, to which he seemed to have satisfactory answers, we told him that the results of the work so far were so striking and would no doubt cause so big a sensation when published, that we felt that it might even be desirable to repeat the whole study in order to see whether the answers came out the same.' Doll was not keen[18] although he recognised that doing the same work in a rural area could be 'very interesting'. The sequel does not appear in the files at the PRO and I am indebted to Sir Richard himself for it. 'Himsworth, who was impressed by our paper,' he writes[19], 'pointed out that the subjects were nearly all Londoners and that the findings were so important that we ought to check that they could be reproduced in other parts of the UK. This we agreed to do and made arrangements to interview patients in Bristol, Cambridge, Leeds, and Newcastle. Before this extension was completed, however, Wynder and Graham published their findings in the USA (June 1950)[20], so we felt justified in publishing ours, which we did a few months later.'[21]

Ernst Wynder and Evarts Graham had conducted a case-control study of similar size and equally conclusive results to Doll and Hill's. Thus by the end of 1950 two substantial studies, one in Britain and one in America, had established beyond reasonable doubt that the alarming rise in lung cancer was due to smoking. Other papers published in America showed similar results. [22]

But publication, so far from causing the predicted sensation, passed almost unnoticed in the press and totally unnoticed on the files (as preserved) of the Medical Research Council and the Ministry of Health.

Notes

1. PRO file FD 1.3567

2. 'Points of View': *Cure of Tobacco Smoking*, The Lancet, 6 September 1952

3. Dr Charles Fletcher took part in this programme, broadcast by the BBC on 12 January 1953. The producer wrote a week earlier to F H K Green at the MRC observing that Imperial Tobacco had 'declined the offer of a chance to put their viewpoint in the same programme - perhaps wisely'. The programme lodged in the political memory: it was referred to in the briefing for Lord Salisbury at the Home Affairs Committee in February 1954 - PRO file FD 1.2009.

4. PRO file FD 1.4761

5. Sir Richard Doll describes Rock Carling in 1946 as 'a central figure in everything to do with cancer and radiation' (personal communication, 19 January 1998). He chaired several MRC committees concerned with cancer and radiotherapy and had been a member of the MRC during the war years.

6. Sir Richard Doll records that Kennaway and Mellanby were attracted by the idea that smoking was to blame, while Stocks was 'convinced that atmospheric pollution was responsible' - Statistical Methods in Medical Research 1998; **7**: 87-117

7. PRO file FD 1.1989

8. PRO file FD 1.1993

9. About this time Dr A H Gale, a Medical Officer in the Ministry of Health, noted that the Kennaways had published in the British Journal of Cancer (1947; **1**: 260-298 - September 1947) an analysis of death certificates: 'The authors suggest tentatively that their findings are consistent with the hypothesis that the inhalation of cigarette smoke may be an aetiological factor [for lung cancer]' - PRO file MH 55.1011.

10. MRC 47/366, PRO file FD 1.1990

11. MRC 47/460, PRO file FD 1.1989

12. MRC 47/502, PRO file FD 1.1989

13. PRO file T 161.1302

14. PRO file T 171.792

15. PRO files T 233.221, T 171.792. The need to reduce dollar imports and the need not to risk revenue from tobacco again came into conflict in 1952, when the Cabinet, with Winston Churchill as Prime Minister in the chair, decided to postpone purchases of 20 million pounds of tobacco from 1952 to 1953. The Cabinet minutes for 6 March 1952 record: 'This would save £4¾ million in dollars for the time being. While there was much to be said on social grounds for a general reduction in tobacco consumption, overseas expenditure on tobacco was small by comparison with the very heavy yield of internal revenue which it produced. If this were not maintained it would be necessary for the Exchequer to absorb purchasing power by other means.'

16. PRO file FD 1.1989

17. PRO file FD 1.1992

18. PRO file FD 1.1992

19. Personal communication, 23 October 1996

20. JAMA 1950; **143**: 329-336

21. BMJ 1950; **ii**: 739-748. 'These published results were essentially those we had shown Himsworth the year before. By the time of publication we had of course preliminary confirmative findings from other parts of the UK and Wynder and Graham's work.' (Sir Richard Doll, personal communication, 23 October 1996).

22. Schrek *et al*, Cancer Research 1950; **10**: 49-58; Levin *et al*, JAMA 1950; **143**: 336-338; Mills *et al*, Cancer Research 1950; **10**: 539-542. For a summary of the results of this research and for the general history of the research on smoking, see Richard Doll's review in Statistical Methods in Medical Research 1998; **7**: 87-117.

1

1951-54:
Pressure for a Government
Statement

D r Horace Joules was Medical Director at the Central Middlesex
County Hospital and already a member of the Central Health Services
Council (CHSC) when in December 1948 the Council appointed him
one of its representatives on the Standing Advisory Committee
(Cancer and Radiotherapy), one of several such standing committees that
advised the Minister of Health, through the CHSC, on a variety of topics.[1]
Richard Doll and Austin Bradford Hill's report in the *British Medical Journal*
might have caused barely a public ripple, but it did not escape Joules' attention,
and he brought it to the notice of the Committee (hereafter 'SAC(CR)') at their
meeting on 18 January 1951. He suggested that the Ministry of Health conduct
a publicity campaign about the dangers of smoking. The SAC(CR), chaired by
Sir Ernest Rock Carling, 'a life-long heavy smoker now in his late 70s'[2], rejected
the idea: this was only 'a preliminary report' and it would be 'premature to base
conclusions on it.' The SAC(CR) agreed at least that the Medical Research
Council should be investigating the matter.[3]

Sir John Charles, the Chief Medical Officer since 1950, accordingly
wrote to Harold Himsworth, the MRC Secretary, asking about its 'committee'
on lung cancer, which had apparently 'not recently been active'. Himsworth
replied that there was no such committee, only a working party set up after the
two original conferences to supervise the 'clinical-statistical investigation' by
Bradford Hill and Doll and the laboratory experiments by Sir Ernest

- 11 -

Kennaway. He reacted strongly to the SAC(CR)'s 'doubts as to the validity of the findings of Bradford Hill and Doll. I find it difficult to understand on what scientific grounds your Committee's opinion could be based, because it has been said of this work . . . that it is 'the best practical lead we have ever had in cancer research'; though I might qualify that by pointing to mulespinners' and chimney-sweeps' cancer, I certainly think that their work has this degree of significance. It is a point perhaps not devoid of interest in relation to any proposal for organising centrally directed publicity on the subject, that the national press (for reasons which can be guessed) almost completely ignored the Hill and Doll report . . .'

'Hill and Doll are satisfied,' Himsworth wrote, 'that the case against smoking as such is proven, and that no further statistical inquiry on the general aspect of that problem is necessary', though they were pursuing more detailed investigations. Himsworth ended by saying that the MRC had 'already organised a statistically conclusive investigation' while laboratory work by Sir Ernest Kennaway was 'in active progress'.

Green's brief, on which Himsworth had based his reply, reveals that the tribute to the work by Bradford Hill and Doll came from Kennaway himself. It also reported:

> Doll tells me privately that he has heard from Joules that the negative attitude taken up by the Minister's Standing Advisory Committee on Cancer, to which Charles refers, depended on a reluctance by some of the members of the Committee to condemn smoking for personal reasons, or because of a supposed possible adverse effect of a decrease in cigarette-smoking upon the National budget, through loss of taxation. If there is any suggestion that the Minister's Committee is really influenced by considerations of this kind, I am sure you will agree that we ought to take a very firm line in endorsing the view of Kennaway, Hill and Doll that the positive correlation between smoking and cancer of the lung is proven, whether we like it or not. I think it important, moreover, that our two cancer conferences should be given due credit for starting a very active and fruitful programme of investigation, instead of being talked about, by those who should know better, as if they were abortive.[4]

The SAC(CR), which met twice a year, considered the MRC's reply in July 1951. The Committee was unconvinced: its

> view remained that the investigations . . . had not produced evidence of a direct relation between smoking and carcinoma of the lung. It was known that there was an increase in smoking and an increase in the incidence of carcinoma of the lung and there was evidence from Dr Doll and Dr Bradford Hill that patients with cancer of the lung had been heavy smokers but no direct evidence of a certain relationship. From discussions the individual members had had with

Dr Bradford Hill it was not thought that he would agree with the Secretary of the Medical Research Council in saying that the case against smoking as such was proven. It was felt that in spite of what the Secretary of the M.R.C. had said, the M.R.C. should carry out further investigations on the relationship.

The SAC(CR) was therefore able, doubtless with some relief, to decide again that a Ministerial publicity campaign would not be justified.[5]

The same month, Austin Bradford Hill wrote to Himsworth setting out his plans for 'a 'forward' inquiry . . . This would involve taking individuals with known smoking histories and then seeing over the next few years, say 5, how they die off, both from cancer of the lung and from other causes.' He reported the 75% response to a trial random sample of 200 names from the medical register, one of whom had by chance been Himsworth himself, and suggested that with 60,000 persons on the register a sample of 40-45,000 answers might be obtained. The BMA would handle the mailing 'without reference to itself', and the Registrar-General had agreed to report all deaths of doctors. The cost would be £1,800: 'This, I regret to say, is considerably more than the sum I mentioned to you personally for in that I was including only the postage involved; I (professorially) forgot that I should first have to print something to send by post and buy envelopes to put it in! The cost of paper is so great today.'

The sum was approved and Landsborough Thomson, now the MRC's Second Secretary, wrote to Bradford Hill, mentioning the increased estimate and the MRC's difficult budgetary position. This elicited a handwritten note from Hill from his Buckinghamshire home expressing contrition[6] but saying he believed 'the inquiry may give a good return in other respects too than cancer of the lung, for the heart diseases may prove interesting.' The circular to doctors was then issued, explaining the reason for selecting doctors for the study: 'The population most likely to be willing to assist in such an inquiry and to give accurate information is clearly one trained in observation and appreciative of the value of research - namely the medical profession.'[7]

In the SAC(CR), Horace Joules returned to the fray in January 1952. 'Since he first raised this matter he had seen 40 cases of cancer of the lung in his hospital, not one of whom had been in the habit of smoking less than 25 cigarettes a day.' The SAC(CR) conceded a request for the opinions of Dr Bradford Hill and Sir Ernest Kennaway. These were accordingly obtained: a minute by an anonymous civil servant in the Ministry of Health comments that Joules 'is as you know the main protagonist against smoking - on the CHSC, on the SAC(CR) and in the Press'. Sir Ernest reported little progress: 'No specific carcinogenic substance, except arsenic, has been identified as yet in tobacco smoke' (there were reasons for doubting the importance of arsenic in the inquiry). Bradford Hill said he had nothing as yet to add to the 1950 article in the *BMJ* pending results from the study of doctors: there was a 'real association' between smoking and lung cancer, but it was not necessarily causal.

Joules was unable to attend the SAC(CR) in June but wrote in strong terms to his colleagues:

> Since I first raised this matter, eighteen months ago, approximately 20,000 people have died from this disease. Some of the most respected citizens of the realm are included in this number . . . I wish to make this last appeal to the committee, to ensure that young people in this country are made aware of the risk of excessive smoking. Surely this is the least we can do in the face of the ever increasing number of deaths. The replies of successive ministers to questions on this matter show they are relying on this committee for medical help. So far I feel we have failed to give this and I trust this state of affairs will not continue. Should the committee not feel able to give this advice I hope this letter can be inserted in the minutes as I do not feel that my protest should pass unrecorded.

Influenced perhaps by the reference to the deaths of 'most respected citizens' - without doubt Joules intended King George VI, a heavy smoker, who had died of a heart attack after an operation for lung cancer in February 1952 - the SAC(CR) began to move. It still held that the evidence was 'insufficient to justify propaganda' but it officially advised the Minister that 'the statistical evidence at present available strongly suggests that there is an association between smoking and cancer of the lung' and the Minister should publicly admit the probability of the relationship. The minutes record: 'A proposed amendment to insert 'excessive' before 'smoking' was not carried.'

Seeing the minutes, Joules wrote to the SAC(CR) secretary asking rhetorically what evidence would be 'sufficient to justify propaganda to prevent this ever increasing mortality', and with hindsight we obviously agree. But it is notable that at the same meeting the SAC(CR) cautiously amended advice it had given the Minister in 1949 'that it was undesirable at the present time for any cancer publicity to be carried out by any central government organisation direct to the general public' by suggesting that he

> should encourage local authorities and voluntary bodies to carry out exploratory schemes of cancer education to enlarge the knowledge of what can be done in this field and that there should be further facilities for educating doctors and medical students in the early recognition of cancer.[8]

The horror of cancer at the time led to its being virtually unmentionable; doctors had few methods to combat the disease and little advice to give about avoiding it; and the Ministry of Health was worried that education would lead to public panic. A 1955 review of policy says it was thought unwise 'to make the public cancer-conscious by fear'.[9] Mild leaflets about cancer from New

Zealand and the USA were obtained early in 1952 but minutes on the file show that their like was unthinkable in the UK, while the official who acted as secretary to the SAC(CR) wrote to a Senior Publicity Assistant in the Ministry, Miss B Crawter, that 'some members of the SAC(CR) are strongly opposed to any cancer education of the public'. In April William Shepherd MP (Conservative, Cheadle) wrote to the Parliamentary Secretary at the Ministry of Health, Patricia Hornsby-Smith, following up a Parliamentary Question that had suggested such education. He said that he did not 'for one moment suggest that there should be a publicity campaign about the dangers of smoking in relation to lung cancer' - only education about 'more general aspects of the disease - such as the recognition of certain symptoms . . . '[10]

The SAC(CR)'s cautious advice to the Minister was forwarded in October to the CHSC, where Dr Joules (as a Ministry minute reveals) 'instigated' the Council to refer it back to the SAC(CR) for reconsideration.[11]

Before the SAC(CR) met again events had moved on apace - but not towards public propaganda. In August the tobacco industry made its entrance to the debate. In 1952 the Imperial Tobacco Company, a highly respectable enterprise with the connections that might be expected of the dominant company in an industry that generated over 14% of the Government's tax revenues, had about 80% of the market in the United Kingdom, and it was Imperial Tobacco that made the move. The first contact was plainly with the Ministry of Health, although no trace remains on the files, for we find Dr Green of the MRC confirming to Dr Neville M Goodman, the Senior Medical Officer in the Ministry responsible for cancer, that he had

> mentioned to Himsworth on Saturday that 'someone high up in the Imperial Tobacco Company Ltd' would probably call on him in September to discuss a scheme of cancer research. He was very interested to hear this, but we are both a little disturbed at the thought that you may inadvertently have given the intending visitor the idea that the Council are not themselves interested in receiving benefactions for medical research

- an idea that he asked Goodman to correct. Goodman replied that the company seemed to want 'to repeat on a larger scale the Doll-Hill inquiry, in which they claim to find many flaws' and to do so without the participation of Doll who, they hinted, 'seemed to have made up his mind on the subject'.

This led to a meeting on 9 October 1952 between Imperial Tobacco and the MRC. The company was represented by its secretary, E J (John) Partridge, and D A Clark, an economist in his office, the MRC by Himsworth (now Sir Harold), Green and Landsborough Thomson. Green's note reports that 'Mr Partridge . . . explained that his firm were naturally unhappy about the suggested association between cigarette smoking and cancer. They were doubtful about the statistical validity . . .' of the published study, but they 'seemed a little disconcerted when we told them that a further paper dealing with the interrogation of 2,500 patients with cancer of the lung and 2,500 controls was to be published by Hill and Doll in the British Medical Journal in December; this paper had the same general conclusions as its predecessor. . .'[12]

The company was clearly at this stage unsure how to react to the threat to the industry. Partridge talked of putting up money for a new study and was invited to make proposals, but at a further meeting later in the same month (at which Dr Goodman took the place of Landsborough Thomson) Partridge said that Imperial was no longer interested in re-running the Doll/Hill study although they would like to discuss their doubts about it with its authors. He agreed first to submit a memorandum. Partridge then 'said that his firm were considering starting independent experimental work' on similar lines to the experimental laboratory work the MRC had commissioned and 'they would welcome the advice of Sir Ernest Kennaway and of other established experts in the field . . .' However, when it was suggested that one helpful step would be to second one of their chemists, even part-time, as an assistant to Sir Ernest Kennaway, 'Mr Partridge was rather doubtful as to whether the firm would have a chemist to spare . . .'

Partridge wrote immediately to Goodman with six pages of objections to the statistical validity of the Doll/Hill study (these concerned the selection of the control sample, the accuracy of self-reports of smoking habits, the lack of rural inhabitants and other matters) and on 30 October Green forwarded his letter to Bradford Hill, commenting:

> He seems to have set [his points] out fairly and reasonably. . . but I think you will have no great difficulty in answering him. He is, of course, in the sad position of not wanting his doubts to be resolved, but, with that limitation, I do think he is making a serious effort to look at the prospect with an unbiased eye. He is certainly a very nice man.

The event was a meeting a week later at the London School of Hygiene and Tropical Medicine between Imperial Tobacco Company, represented by Partridge, Clark and Geoffrey Todd, their statistician, and Bradford Hill, Doll and Green from the MRC, who kept a record and commented:[13]

> The meeting was very friendly . . . It was pretty clear to me that Mr Partridge and his colleagues felt that Hill had answered all their queries in a way which left hardly any loophole for doubt, though they were naturally reluctant to concede this . . .

and Green was obviously appreciative of the way the researchers performed, as can be seen from his letter of 7 November to Bradford Hill, which has to be quoted in full, 'Dear Tony,' he wrote:

I send you these cigars in grateful (if ironical) appreciation of your tactful handling of the tobacconists yesterday, and in gratitude also for your advice, help and hospitality over many years.

I hope they are tolerable and have sufficiently matured (I know little about such things). I hope much more, of course, that they do not plunge you, of all people, into the equivocal but dangerous category of a 'heavy smoker' - but I hardly suppose there are enough of them for that.

Yours ever . . .

Bradford Hill's reaction is not recorded - but cigars were not covered by the questionnaire sent to doctors[14] and for long were regarded as relatively innocuous.

At the end of January Partridge sent a new, expanded version of Todd's statistical objections, and in February responded to a request from Green with a form of words that the MRC could use to report the meetings to the SAC(CR):

We have had informal discussions with Tobacco Manufacturers on this matter. They consider that the evidence . . . is far from conclusive and that there is a considerable weight of evidence against the existence of such a correlation. In their view there is no proof whatever of any causal connection.

The Manufacturers have assured us, however, that they have a full sense of the importance of the problem. They have in hand a programme of chemical research into the constituents of tobacco and tobacco smoke which was started some time ago in order to obtain information required for general trade purposes. They are intensifying the aspects of this research that will throw light on the problem now under discussion and all their resources will be used to complete this work in the shortest possible space of time.

The Manufacturers will keep in touch with biological and other research which is being carried on in other Institutions and will cooperate whenever possible with research workers engaged in these fields.

The SAC(CR) met on 5 February 1953. The MRC reported on the work it was sponsoring: Sir Ernest Kennaway hoped to make progress now that he had managed to borrow from the Eastern Gas Board an assistant to do spectroscopic and chromatographic analyses; Dr P R Peacock at Royal Beatson Memorial Hospital, Glasgow, had failed to find benzpyrene or other known carcinogens in tobacco smoke, although claims had been published of carcinogenic effects in mice.[15] A paper from the SAC(CR) secretary reported:

> The Imperial Tobacco Company has requested that a paper prepared by one of their statisticians and entitled 'The statistical study of Tobacco Smoke in relation to the aetiology of Carcinoma of the Lung' should be submitted to the Committee'

but (he wrote) the paper was long and technical and would be circulated later with 'an expert statistical opinion . . .' The SAC(CR) was provided with Todd's own summary:

> The argument of this paper is that if tobacco is . . . a factor [in the production of cancer of the lung] then it must have been so over a period of time and consequently that it would be a fair test of the validity of the hypothesis to apply the current risk of death from lung cancer, induced by causes connected with smoking - assuming that such causes exist - to the population at risk in earlier periods and to see if the theoretically expected deaths, after making allowances for deaths from cancer of the lung from causes not connected with smoking, approximate to the recorded deaths. Judged by this test, the hypothesis is untrue.
>
> It is then considered whether there is any reason why the hypothesis should be valid at the present time but not in earlier years, and it is concluded that the hypothesis could only be true now if some changes in other factors had turned tobacco from an innocuous substance into one which is now a factor in the production of cancer of the lung. No such change has in fact been demonstrated.

The paper went on to contest two of the assumptions made by Bradford Hill and Doll.

The SAC(CR) had a confused discussion. Horace Joules referred to the new paper by Doll and Bradford Hill which reported that risk 'increased with age and in simple arithmetical proportion to the amount smoked'. The public anxiety and press attention meant that the 'Ministry should arrange for authoritative information to be given to the medical profession and to the public'. He won some support, but the meeting ended with a decision to circulate the Imperial Tobacco paper and 'meet again shortly' - or, as a correction to the minutes won by Joules had it, 'within a month'.[16] The minutes might say so, but the SAC(CR) did not in fact meet again until November.

That same day (5 February) Goodman, the Medical Officer at the Ministry, brought Partridge and Clark to visit Green at the MRC. They sought an early reaction to Todd's paper, which they hoped (they said) to see published in the *BMJ*[17]. Partridge reported that Todd was inclined to see as 'derogatory to himself' the idea that the SAC(CR) might seek independent advice on his paper and those by Doll and Hill. 'I [Green] said that it seemed to me that he had much less to complain of in this respect than Professor Bradford Hill and Dr Doll. . . Mr Partridge accepted this point of view.'

Partridge said that his chairman (Sir Robert Sinclair) was considering whether to mention the controversy over smoking and health at the company AGM and read a rough draft of a possible statement.[18] He also asked for suggestions whom to ask for advice on planning 'biological experiments on the constituents of tobacco smoke' and Green provided names.[19]

This was typical of - very frequent - dealings between the company and the Ministry and MRC at this time: the impression yielded by the papers is that everyone was facing a problem together; there were different emphases (the AGM draft 'erred in the direction of too emphatically denying the validity of the Hill and Doll evidence, but otherwise it seemed to me harmless for its purpose') but a solution needed to be found cooperatively if not in collaboration. So, Green provided an introduction for Imperial to the MRC's Pneumoconiosis Research Unit in Cardiff (where, a report to the SAC(CR) at this time revealed, Dr B M Wright 'is examining, with an ingenious apparatus of his own invention, the effect on mice of living for long periods in a heavy atmosphere of tobacco smoke').

Five days later Partridge provided a revised version of Todd's paper, and a further revision came the following week (and another in June); on 2 March Bradford Hill sent Green his response, and on 9 March Partridge sent Todd's rejoinder.

At this point the paper (running to over 30 pages), response and rejoinder were circulated to the SAC(CR), along with a letter published in the *British Medical Journal*[20] from Dr R D Passey, Professor of Experimental Pathology and Director of Cancer Research, University of Leeds, which is worth quoting. Dr Passey's letter pointed out that lung cancer had increased in parallel with not only the growth of cigarette smoking but also the ability to diagnose the disease. No carcinogenic agent had yet been found in tobacco smoke, let alone been shown to be capable of producing lung cancer. Often in the past correlations had led to false assumptions of cause: for example 'In the early years of the present century it was taught, and it was in the students' textbooks, that breast cancer might be related to the bone and metal supports of the corsets of the Edwardian days; but in the intervening 45 years the incidence of mammary cancer has not fallen.' If smoking caused lung cancer, why did it not also cause cancer of the mouth, tongue and pharynx? 'In point of fact, there is some slight decrease in these sites.' He continued:

> In the early 'thirties it was the fashion to ascribe lung cancer to the tarring of the roads and to the exhaust fumes of motor vehicles, but the failure to demonstrate any higher incidence in those specially exposed to such hazards resulted in the abandonment of the

hypothesis. Then the traces of arsenic in British tobaccos received the blame, but that belief, too, has been discredited. The industrial pollution of the air we breathe has been considered a factor, in spite of the fact that, while lung cancer figures are rising, the aerial pollution is definitely decreasing. When doctors disagree it is bad for the patient.

It may be that a proportion of lung cancers in man are induced by tobacco smoking: at the moment we do not know, but let us be sure of our evidence before we scare our public. As a profession we have that responsibility.

Meanwhile Sir John Charles, the Chief Medical Officer, had asked Percy Stocks, now Senior Research Fellow of the British Empire Cancer Campaign, to suggest referees for the conflicting papers. Stocks suggested names, including the Government Actuary, Sir George Maddex KBE, who in the event chaired the panel, but in his reply he commented:

In reading [Todd] I was struck by the absence of any appreciation of the long period of time which must elapse between the initiation of the malignant process in the lung and death resulting from it, which suggests that it has been written by a non-medical statistician. If the average period is 15 or 20 years, as it probably is, the argument in parts I-III and the statistical method applied appears to me to be nonsense, since it presupposes deaths to occur in the same year as the cancer was initiated.

Sir John Charles replied by return, asking what evidence there was for the 15-20 year development period:

Surely this is in great part an assumption, based on the analogy of the activities of skin cancer. If, however, there is actual evidence other than that I have mentioned in support of the thesis, could you let me know what it is?

Stocks pointed out in reply:

The evidence in favour of a long induction period of 15-20 years for lung cancer is not based only on analogy with the action of carcinogenic agents whose nature and induction period is known, such as the chemicals affecting the bladder and skin. There is also internal evidence from the findings in Doll & Hill's investigations, which show, for example, that 98 per cent of the men with lung cancer who had smoked began to smoke before the age of 30, but nevertheless 90 per cent were over 45 when cancer was diagnosed. How can this be explained unless either the carcinogenic poison was gradually accumulating in the body for 15 years or more in most cases before the malignant process began, or else the malignant process took that time in most cases to develop to the stage when it could be diagnosed?

Further, he argued, those who smoked less, although at less risk, did not seem to get lung cancer later, indicating that there was a prolonged latency period.

Parliament had taken little interest in the debate about smoking and did not begin to put pressure on Ministers for another two years. However, Harry Hynd MP (Labour, Accrington) gave notice in March 1953 that he would raise the matter in an adjournment debate. The preparation of the Minister's brief reveals that the Ministry's caution attracted criticism from the MRC. Dr Goodman at the Ministry recorded: 'We must clearly remain completely uncommitted, since we genuinely do not know at present whether tobacco smoking - and particularly heavy tobacco smoking - is a causal factor . . .' He conceded that it was accepted 'generally, but not universally' that a statistical link between smoking and lung cancer had been proved, but it was not necessarily causal. The SAC(CR) needed time to consider Todd's criticisms of the statistics, the inconclusive laboratory attempts to find carcinogens in tobacco smoke, the alternative hypotheses (he mentions atmospheric pollution, road tar and exhaust fumes) and other matters.

The draft brief was sent to the MRC for comment and Green, after consulting Himsworth, wrote back: 'We both feel that in an effort to be cautious the compiler of the brief has been unfair to Hill and Doll', whose work was planned and extended, not 'based on impressions and prejudices'. It was 'improper' for the brief to suggest that their statistical evidence could be 'lightly discounted'. The brief remained cautious, however, and the speech notes for Patricia Hornsby-Smith, the junior health minister who replied to the debate, say: 'Cannot accept even this report [i.e., Hill & Doll] without further enquiry: statistical evidence of association - not universally accepted . . .' The Minister was subsequently criticised by a Miss Mary Baker who wrote from the Morton Hotel in Russell Square to say: 'It hardly behoves the Ministry of Health to be two years behind the times on a matter that has lately aroused so much public interest . . .'[21]

Sir George Maddex was now commissioned, along with other distinguished statisticians[22], to study the work of Bradford Hill and Doll and the criticisms by Todd and Passey. The panel questioned both Todd and Hill and Doll, having given them notice of the intended lines of questioning, and they received further late amendments to his paper from Todd. On 12 November, Sir George submitted their report to Sir John Charles, and it was promptly circulated to the SAC(CR) in whose name it had been commissioned.

The report runs to five pages, with appendices drawn from the papers submitted to the panel, some of them additional analysis by Hill and Doll of their original results. The report is moderately worded but decisive. 'We have carefully considered the criticisms Todd has made of the conduct of the investigation. We have come to the conclusion that Doll and Hill took every practicable care to avoid possible introduction of bias into their results and that, so far as we can see, they have been successful . . . We are therefore of the opinion that the main conclusion reached by Doll and Hill, that there is a real association between smoking and cancer of the lung, is firmly established.' Although the relationship was not proven to be causal, 'all the other possible explanations we can think of are ruled out by the careful matching of lung cancer cases and controls. There is therefore a strong presumption . . . that the connexion between smoking and lung cancer is causal.' However, Todd's analysis showed that it was unlikely that the whole increase in lung cancer over the past 30 years was due to smoking, and the panel was cautious about Doll's calculations of risk.[23]

The SAC(CR) met on 23 November. The minutes record its conclusion:

> The evidence was sufficient to justify advising the Minister that the association was real and that the Panel's suggestion that the association was causal was acceptable. Young persons should be warned of the risk attendant on smoking and it should be made clear that the risk apparently increased in proportion to the amount of tobacco smoked. The risk from cigarette smoking was apparently greater than from other forms of smoking.

It was decided that a draft of the advice to be given to the Minister should be put to the following meeting. A note to the members of Sir George's panel with which each was sent his own duplicated copy of the report mentions the 'considerable impression' it made on the SAC(CR) 'many of whose members as a result changing *(sic)* the views they have previously held on the subject. The last has certainly not been heard of the question.'

The SAC(CR) might have been moved, but there were those in the Ministry who had not. Over the next few days Medical Officers and officials sent each other minutes about the drafting of the advice the SAC(CR) should be recommended to give the Minister. M R P Gregson, an Assistant Secretary, discussed the matter with Sir Ernest Rock Carling, the chairman of the SAC(CR), who had been (Gregson's minute records) the sole dissentient at the SAC(CR)'s meeting (he 'feels that the evidence is insufficiently conclusive'). They concluded that 'the recommendation, if it is to be any way acceptable to the Committee in their present mood, will have to stress . . . (i) reality of the association, (ii) the presumption of causality, and (iii) the justification for warning the younger generation.' Gregson provides a draft:

> That an association between smoking and cancer of the lung has been established and, in the absence of evidence to the contrary, there is a strong presumption that the relationship is causal. Whilst further research is needed to establish the presence and nature of the carcinogen and the extent to which it operates, there is an obligation, in view of this presumption, to warn young people of the risks attendant on smoking, risks which are apparently proportionate to the

amount of tobacco smoked. While the risks from cigarettes seem to be greater than those from any other form of smoking, it is not possible to state any number of cigarettes below which the risk can be disregarded.

Two days later, after he has spoken to Dr Goodman, who in turn consulted the CMO, he provides a new draft that takes account of the CMO's suggestion that it be 'toned down a bit'. So 'there is an obligation . . . to warn young people' becomes 'it is desirable . . . that young people should be warned', and the lack of a safe threshold is omitted altogether.

The next day further comments from the CMO, Sir John Charles, are passed on to Gregson: 'The objection to this draft is that it does not sufficiently take account of the qualifications (other factors, qualifying phrases, etc.) contained in the Maddex report'. The next draft is half as long again; the presumption of causality is now to be made not 'in the absence of evidence to the contrary' but only 'until some positive evidence to the contrary is found'. And stress is laid on the 'other factor or factors' that may be at play and the 'further research' that is needed.[24] More drafts ensue, and finally the version put to the SAC(CR) is as follows (italics added for ease of later reference):

(1)   It must be regarded as established that there is a real relationship between smoking and cancer of the lung.

(2)   Though there is a strong presumption, *until the contrary is shown*, that the relationship is causal, there is evidence that the relationship is not a simple one, since:-

(a)   the evidence in support of the presence in tobacco smoke of a carcinogenic agent causing cancer of the lung is not yet certain;

(b)   the statistical evidence indicates that it is unlikely that the *real* increase in the incidence of cancer of the lung is due entirely to increases in smoking;

(c)   the differences in incidence between urban and rural areas, and between different towns, suggest that other factors may be operating, e.g., atmospheric pollution, occupational risks;

(d)   *the effect of smoking may be dependent on the presence of other constitutional factors common to those who smoke and those who develop cancer of the lung.*

(3)   *In view of the probable existence of other factors, no reliable quantitative estimates can be made of the effect of smoking on the incidence of cancer of the lung.*

(4)   Although no dramatic fall in death-rates could be expected if smoking ceased, since the development of lung cancer may be the result of factors operating over many years, it is desirable that young

people should be warned of the risks apparently attendant on excessive smoking.

The SAC(CR) met on 22 December 1953 to consider this suggested advice to the Minister. Members recognised the need for caution but found the draft 'hedged around by too many qualifications'. They omitted the words italicised above and amended the final paragraph to add back that risk appeared proportionate to the amount smoked[25], but the advice they adopted was still substantially weaker than they clearly had had in mind at their previous meeting. 'The Standing Committee was at first disposed to accept extreme views and advised the Minister to take some sort of dramatic action', notes a Ministry Undersecretary in January 1954, but 'under the influence of [the draft prepared in the Ministry] a rather more moderate conclusion was reached'.[26]

Horace Joules was plainly dissatisfied: a minute on the Ministry file records that 'the Chairman mentioned that the Committee's advice would automatically go to the CHSC [Central Health Services Council] (and he told Dr Joules that he would have another chance of raising the matter there).' But Joules' days on the SAC(CR) were numbered: he had rocked the boat too much. A minute on the file records that his appointment was due to expire on 31 March 1954. 'Dr Joules was originally suggested by the Department, but his reappointment has not been supported by any of the organisations we consult.'[27] His replacement, Dr Janet Aitken, in accepting the invitation, wrote to the Minister: 'I am not really an expert from a medical point of view in cancer and radiotherapy'.[28]

The Minister, Iain Macleod, pre-empted the CHSC, deciding that a statement had to be made without delay.[29] But first the tobacco industry intervened again. Dr Goodman, the Medical Officer at the Ministry, had had a meeting on 28 October 1953 with Dr E L Wynder, the leading researcher in the USA and co-author of the study that (as recorded above) prompted immediate publication of their results by Doll and Hill:

> He is a young man 'far gone in enthusiasm' for the causal relationship between tobacco smoking and lung cancer. (I had been told when I was in New York this spring that he was the son of a revivalist preacher and had inherited his father's antipathy to tobacco and alcohol. The American Cancer Society were very suspicious of his early work for this reason.)

Wynder, however, had talked of the 'large grants' the American industry had made for research:

> He said that the American Tobacco Companies were anxious that parallel research should go on in this country and were prepared to make funds available to any 'neutral' body which would undertake it, e.g., the Ministry of Health. I told him that I thought the Medical

Research Council were the proper body to approach in the first place . . .

The minute was copied to Dr Green at the MRC, who commented:

> Dr Goodman's slightly 'sour' minute about his talk with Dr Wynder seems to me symptomatic of the great reluctance of the Ministry's M.O.s to accept what we regretfully believe to be the 'facts of life (and death)' on smoking and lung cancer . . . The news about the plans of the American tobacco firms is interesting, if true.[30]

On 18 December, Sir Alexander Maxwell, who occupied an ambiguous position between the tobacco industry and the Board of Trade[31], handed to Sir Harold Himsworth, the MRC Secretary, a memorandum rehearsing the industry's doubts about the link between smoking and lung cancer but making an offer of £250,000 - over £4 mn in 1999 money - over seven years 'for specific research into the real cause of cancer of the lung. Such research would, of course, embrace other possible factors besides smoking.' Maxwell signed the memorandum as chairman of the Tobacco Advisory Committee 'on behalf of the leading U.K. Tobacco Manufacturers'.

News of this offer reached the Ministry of Health during its consideration of the SAC(CR)'s formal advice to the Minister. J E Pater, now an undersecretary (and remembered by Sir George Godber as 'a steady pipe smoker'[32]), prepared a three-page minute, with annexes, which went through the Chief Medical Officer to the Minister. Pater advised that 'any kind of propaganda campaign' would be 'premature until there is a good deal more reliable evidence', but that a statement of the SAC(CR)'s advice would be 'reasonable'. He saw merit in an early statement before the CHSC met, since 'on past experience, any modification made by the Central Health Services Council on this subject is more likely to be unhelpful than helpful'. But by-passing the CHSC would require 'an urgent reason', such as perhaps a Parliamentary Question if one were put down. (If not, he saw no alternative to awaiting the CHSC, since he would scruple to take the 'rather dubious step' of arranging for a Question to be asked.)

It was left to the deputy secretary I F (later Sir Frederick) Armer, to advise that a two-month delay in revealing the SAC(CR)'s important advice might be open to criticism. Iain Macleod agreed: 'This, of course, is a problem that we have seen coming for a long time and is one that requires very delicate public relations handling'. He rejected delay and asked for a paper to be prepared 'at once' for the Cabinet Home Affairs Committee.

The paper[33] was issued four days later. The first draft had said: '. . . the statistical evidence leaves no doubt that there is a causal relationship between smoking and lung cancer, even if we do not know how or to what extent one causes the other' but this was annotated: 'Can we look again at [this] which seems to go just a little too far?' and the final version said nothing so inflammatory. It began by rehearsing the background, quoting the SAC(CR)'s advice, mentioning the tobacco companies' offer to the MRC, and noting that in America the industry had published 'advertisements to the public stating that, while they do not accept a causal relationship, they are financing independent research.'[34] It then proposed making an early statement to the House of Commons but resisting any demand for propaganda.

Before the Committee met, the Treasury asked to be kept informed, and Iain Macleod accordingly wrote to John Boyd-Carpenter, the Financial Secretary:

> . . . I needn't say anything about the financial implications of any ill-considered statement in this field for we all know that the Welfare State and much else is based on tobacco smoking. I would, however, like to make a point here about the political implications of delay. [He explained the risks of criticism if the Ministry delayed publishing the SAC(CR)'s advice.] Moreover, the prime mover in all this is a man [plainly Dr Horace Joules] of extremely advanced left wing opinions[35] and would not hesitate to embarrass the Government if nothing appears soon. The subject is clearly one that the papers are bound to make much of and I need not enlarge on the unfortunate affect *(sic)* that it would have if we were accused in the Press of holding back this sort of information to bolster, as would be suggested, the revenue. My only anxiety is to make whatever statement should be made as quietly as is possible but I feel that we must move soon if events are not to overtake us . . .

Boyd-Carpenter agreed that 'delay should be avoided', and simultaneously Pater advised on 'the latest developments . . . which I have heard from the Treasury. It appears that representatives of the tobacco companies were seen there on Tuesday and were reasonable in their attitude.' The companies had originally wanted no publicity about their offer of cash for research ('presumably because they were fearful that the making of the donation might be publicly interpreted as indicating the implicit acceptance by them of an association between smoking and cancer of the lung'[36]) but had been persuaded that a statement would have to be made. Now the approach of the Imperial Tobacco's company AGM became a factor in deciding the Government's timing. Moreover, their offer obtained for the tobacco companies an inside track on the preparation of the statement: Pater advised that the Treasury wanted the terms of the Minister's statement to 'be agreed with the Treasury and the tobacco companies' (who would be shown the draft by the Treasury) while 'a statement to be made at the same time by the tobacco companies would be agreed with the Treasury, the M.R.C. and ourselves . . .'

The Home Affairs Committee met on Friday 5 February 1954, with the Lord President of the Council, the Marquess of Salisbury, in the chair. The

Lord President oversaw the affairs of the MRC[37], and Sir Harold Himsworth had written to him on 1 February: 'The comments by the tobacco manufacturers . . . have not hitherto been characterised by good sense, dignity or a judicial appraisal of the evidence. It is certain that when the Minister of Health makes his announcement it will elicit a rejoinder and it is to be feared that this may be intemperate.' As a result the MRC might have to publicly disavow what the companies said. Care was therefore needed over the manner of announcement. Sir Harold, indeed, met the tobacco companies on 4 February at the offices of the solicitors through whom they had until then - anonymously - communicated their proposals. He warned them in unequivocal terms of the independence of the MRC and that the Council would not hesitate in case of need to comment 'adversely or otherwise' on any statement from the manufacturers and he gave them the opportunity to withdraw their offer, which they declined.[38]

Lord Salisbury's brief for the Home Affairs Committee from his own office recognised that an announcement 'may well be unavoidable before long . . . But the possible effect of an announcement on the Revenue clearly cannot be ignored. The yield of the tobacco tax is about £600 millions a year - i.e., considerably more than the cost of the Health Service. The television programme about two years ago' - it is revealing that there was nothing more recent to refer to - 'seems to have had little effect on smoking. But it may well be that people paid little attention to that programme, thinking that if the matter was really as serious as was suggested, the Government would have made an announcement. If this were so, the effect of the Minister of Health's announcement might be to bring about a serious reduction in revenue, which it would be very difficult to replace by any tax as little objected to or as easily collected as the tobacco tax. I need hardly say that these considerations are advanced not as an argument against making an announcement if one is considered justified on the merits but as one for weighing all the more carefully the case on merits for making one.'[39]

At the meeting, Macleod made a long opening statement, saying that 'there was no doubt in his own mind that a relationship between tobacco smoking and lung cancer had been established'. He proposed an early statement, timed just before the Imperial AGM, so that the company could then announce the offer to the MRC, which would, however, not meet to consider the offer until later.

The Committee agreed that a statement had to be made, despite the 'serious repercussions on revenue from the tobacco tax' that Boyd-Carpenter noted it might cause. '[T]he announcement should not cause undue alarm by implying that a causal relationship . . . had been clearly established by other methods' than statistics.

A sub-committee was appointed to agree the terms of the statement and to consider how to deal with the tobacco companies' offer: Lord Salisbury had cast doubt on the propriety of the MRC accepting the money, and it had been suggested that it should instead be diverted to the British Empire Cancer Campaign. Boyd-Carpenter, however, was worried that refusing the money might lead to public embarrassment and 'might result in the Government having to put up the money for the research instead'; besides, research commissioned by the BECC would not have the authority conferred by the Government-backed MRC.

Lord Salisbury wrote on 8 February to the Chancellor, R A Butler, seeking his view of the propriety of accepting the donation: the MRC would 'loyally accept' a Cabinet decision to decline it but 'with deep regret . . . £250,000 is a vast sum, and most valuable research could be done with it. It would, moreover, be an immense help to the Council, in their desperate struggle to balance their budget.'[40] Later the same day Boyd-Carpenter later replied with the Chancellor's views, namely that 'it would be a pity to lose the £250,000. On the other hand, he sees the point which I think was troubling you of the doubtful propriety of the M.R.C. accepting direct this money from an outside and highly interested body. He felt therefore that the difficulty could be best got over if the tobacco companies could be persuaded to make the gift to Her Majesty's Government . . .'

The Home Affairs Committee had decided that the matter was serious enough to be reported to the full Cabinet, and a short paper ('the statistical evidence does seem to indicate that there is a causal relationship . . .') was circulated on 8 February[41]. The same day the Minister issued a paper[42] to the new sub-committee, proposing an answer to a planted Parliamentary Question that would quote the SAC(CR)'s advice and conclude:

> I accept the Committee's view that the statistical evidence points to a causal relationship between smoking and lung cancer, but I think it is only right to draw attention to the fact that there is so far no firm evidence of the way in which smoking causes lung cancer or of the extent to which it does so. Any further action must await the results of research into the causes of lung cancer, and this research is being vigorously pursued.

This elicited criticism from Sir Walter Monckton, the Minister of Labour and National Service, who objected that

> the phrase . . . 'the statistical evidence points to a causal relationship' goes a good deal further than [the SAC(CR)'s] view . . . that 'there is a strong presumption that the relationship is causal.

He produced an alternative version to 'reintroduc[e] the element of doubt which the [Standing Advisory] Committee did not feel able to rule out completely':

> I accept the Committee's view that the statistical evidence points to smoking as a factor in the production of lung cancer, but I would draw attention to the fact that there is so far no firm evidence of the way in which smoking may cause lung cancer or of the extent to which it does so. Research into causes of lung cancer has been pressed forward by the Government and by other agencies in view of the increase in the incidence of this disease, and we must look to the results of its vigorous pursuit to determine future action.

When the sub-committee met the next day, Macleod said he 'was happy to accept' Sir Walter's version. Indeed, he said that 'he, accompanied by the Secretary of the Medical Research Council, might give a Lobby Conference on the morning of the 12 February [when the statement was to be made] to try to ensure that press comment on his statement maintained a sense of proportion.'

As to the tobacco companies' 'gift', the sub-committee decided that diverting the money to (for example) the BECC 'might appear to indicate a lack of confidence' in the MRC. It was necessary to 'remove any suggestion of influence being brought to bear' on the MRC but there were doubts about the companies' willingness to give the money to the Government, who would pass it to the MRC, since it would not then get the same tax treatment as a gift to the MRC, a charity. The device the sub-committee produced was that:

> the Secretary of the Medical Research Council should be advised to inform the tobacco companies that the Council could not themselves directly accept the money and that the proper course would be for the companies to approach the Minister of Health for advice as to the proper channel for the gift. The Minister could then advise the companies that the money should be made available to the Medical Research Council and all doubts about the propriety of the gift being accepted would thus be removed.

The proposed Parliamentary Question and answer were reported[43] to the Cabinet at its meeting on 10 February. Macleod said that it was 'desirable that young people should be warned' but repeated that he would 'hold a Lobby Conference with the object of encouraging the Press to maintain a due sense of proportion in their comments on his statement'. Sir Winston Churchill, the Prime Minister, said that the Minister 'should also make public as much as possible of the facts and arguments on which the Standing Advisory Committee had based their advice'.[44]

The lobby conference (actually a press conference) and statement went ahead as agreed. The Ministry issued a three-page briefing paper which subtly emphasised the doubts and uncertainties of the situation while 'paying tribute to the valuable pioneer work of Dr Doll and Professor Bradford Hill and other workers who have given us what little information we have'. In his Parliamentary Answer, the Minister referred to the tobacco companies' gift:

> I should also tell the House that before these recommendations were considered by Her Majesty's Government the tobacco companies had offered to give £250,000 for research. They have, on my advice, agreed to offer this money to the Medical Research Council.

The Parliamentary statement and the briefing paper are reproduced in the Appendix.

The tobacco companies[45] issued a simultaneous statement 'with a full sense of their responsibility to the public'. They referred to the limitations of statistics, the lack of proof that smoking caused lung cancer, and the evidence that other factors had to be at work (some non-smokers contracted the disease while only a 'very small proportion' of smokers contracted it; and it was more common in towns than the country, indicating a possible role for air pollution). They had arranged the previous December to provide £250,000 over seven years for research by 'an impartial and responsible medical body' and on the advice of the Ministry of Health they had asked the MRC to 'undertake this responsibility'.

At the press conference, as the *News Chronicle* noted the next day, Macleod chain-smoked four 'large-size' cigarettes, lighting one from another. Macleod was flanked by Sir John Charles, noted by the press as a non-smoker, and by Sir Harold Himsworth who 'carried a pipe but did not light it' (as the *Daily Telegraph* reported) and who suggested that smoking might become dangerous at a level of more than five cigarettes a day.

The press gave the Minister's statement moderate but passing attention. Macleod's warning against 'uninformed and alarmist conclusions' was widely reported. *The Times* gave its report most of a column on the main news page, opposite the leaders, and devoted its second leader to the subject, one (it said) of 'intense public interest': the implications 'may indeed be serious but, as the Minister has, rightly, been at pains to point out, a proper perspective must be maintained'. It suggested that 'moderation in all things' was the 'soundest rule' pending further research, for financing which the tobacco companies were commended. The *Daily Telegraph* put a short report down a column on its front page with a fuller report inside. Its leader remarked that statistics 'as is well known, can prove anything; and it is perhaps rather arbitrary to infer that smoking is so much responsible for the terrible increase in deaths from cancer of the lung.' (Two days later a diary item recorded that the Chancellor of the Exchequer, R A Butler, had 'exclaimed lightly' at a recent Conservative Party gathering 'For goodness' sake do not stop smoking', adding 'He spoke from the heart'.)

The *News Chronicle, Daily Express* and *Daily Mail* all put small items on page one about tobacco share prices falling sharply, with fuller reports inside, the two first making much of Macleod's chain-smoking. In a leader the *News Chronicle* praised the tobacco companies for their 'due sense of their public responsibilities' and said there was cause for 'concern' but not 'panic'. The *Daily Herald* also put the share price on page one but its inside report, 'by the Herald doctor', did everything possible to play down the risks. The *Daily Mirror* by contrast gave most of its front page to its story predicting '4 New Moves' - all research-related. The *Observer* the next day had a well researched background piece on page one, but the *Sunday Times* made no mention of the story at all and there was little reference to it anywhere in subsequent weeks.

The Ministry files contain none of these cuttings nor any follow-up correspondence. Politically, the issue went into hibernation. The risks of upsetting the public had been carefully avoided without ignoring the troublesome advice of the experts, and the panacea of further research had been applied at no extra expense to the Government.

Notes

1. PRO file MH 133.450. Sir George Godber, then a medical officer at the Ministry of Health (but not responsible for policy on smoking either at this time or until he became Chief Medical Officer), writes: 'Horace Joules was a founding member of the Socialist Medical Association and was appointed to the CHSC by Nye Bevan. He was a good physician and M.S. [medical superintendent] of a good hospital.' (Personal communication, 19 January 1998)

2. I quote Sir George Godber (personal communication, 19 January 1998), who sees Rock Carling's reluctance to act against smoking as sadly out of keeping with his distinguished record, from his service as a surgeon in the Boer War to his pioneering advocacy of radiotherapy.

3. PRO file MH 133.453

4. PRO files MH 55.1011, FD 1.1992

5. PRO file MH 133.453

6. Bradford Hill had forgotten also the labour of opening the 40,000 returned envelopes: in May 1952 he wrote to the MRC recalling a verbal agreement that he pay his sons ('the price being 2/-. a hundred forms opened and scrutinized which is just about an hour's work') and asking for cheques for £12 for one and £13 for the other boy. 'Most of the remainder of the envelopes I opened myself partly as a misguided form of relaxation, partly to inform myself of the

nature of the results; but this, of course, represents a freely offered labour of love.'

7. PRO file FD 1.1992

8. PRO file MH 133.453. A circular was eventually issued to local authorities in August 1953 encouraging them to attempt some health education about cancer in general (PRO file MH 55.960); and in November the Ministry filed a cutting from the East Anglian Daily Times reporting that the Medical Officer of Health for Essex, Dr Kenneth Cowan, had told a rally of scouts and guides at Chelmsford: 'If I were in my adolescence . . . I would never start smoking. I have two pipes and a packet of cigarettes in my pocket, but it is too late for me to really worry, because it takes years and years of smoking to produce a possible serious result.' He urged them to abstain - and at the end of his talk he lit a cigarette. A Ministry annotation in an unidentified hand says: 'Cowan, to my knowledge, is a fairly heavy smoker. This is probably a very good line.' - PRO file MH 55.1011.

9. PRO file MH 55.2220

10. In March 1953, Miss Crawter minuted to her boss, the Public Relations and Chief Press Officer at the Ministry of Health (S A Heald) that she had fended off a proposal in the Central Council for Health Education (a joint local authorities body) to issue a leaflet summarising the facts about smoking. 'It was difficult to discover from whom this desire emanated, other than that "there had been a lot in the press about it"; it seemed to me to be premature and I ventured to remark that the press and the B.B.C. were giving plenty of information, that it was not possible to suggest any positive measure of prevention (since the CCHE did not intend to discourage smoking) and that in my view the proposed leaflet was not health education . . . The matter has been deferred for six months. (I view this suggestion as the CCHE jumping into a controversial matter to boost their sales, and believe that they would have regretted the leaflet in a few months' time, as they might easily have biassed it in a direction which ultimate opinion on the subject would not have supported.' Heald recorded: 'Miss Crawter did well to intervene to kill the leaflet (as much in CCHE's own interest as in the general interest).' PRO files MH 55.959, MH 55.960

11. PRO files MH 55.1011, MH 133.453

12. This paper (BMJ 1952; ii: 1271-86) included the new data from the extended study requested by Himsworth in four other towns (see above) as well as the original data from London.

13. PRO file FD 1.2015. Richard Doll writes (personal communication, 23 October 1996): 'As to our meeting with Partridge & Todd, it was friendly! Todd made three points: (i) that smoking histories were too unreliable to use, (ii) that the correlation between cigarette consumption and lung cancer in different countries was too small, only 0.5, and (iii) that lung cancer was

obviously due to atmospheric pollution. Bradford Hill responded that if smoking histories were unreliable this must have made the association appear weaker than it actually is, that the correlation was unusually high for that sort of data, and that if lung cancer was due to atmospheric pollution, go and show it!'

14.   Sir Richard Doll (personal communication, 23 October 1996) points out that cigars were included in all the later questionnaires, starting in 1957, following reports of low risks in the American case-control studies.

15.   Graham, Wynder & Croninger (*Science*, 14 November 1952) had claimed 'tar from cigarette smoke will produce malignant growths when painted on the skin of mice'; J M Essenberg (Science, 21 November 1952) had reported that prolonged exposure of albino mice to tobacco smoke 'greatly increases the incidence of the primary neoplasms of the lung'.

16.   PRO file references MH 133.453, MH 133.456

17.   They apparently asked Goodman to help them get it accepted: Partridge wrote to him on 9 March saying the paper had been submitted to the journal: 'You may remember that you very kindly promised to have a word with [Hugh] Clegg [editor of the *British Medical Journal*] about publication when we were able to advise you about the despatch of the paper to him.' The attempt was, of course, unsuccessful.

18.   The statement was made at the AGM, on 17 March: '. . . I think it desirable that I should say something about a subject to which a certain amount of public attention has recently been directed - the proposition (which incidentally is founded on a suggested statistical correlation) that in some way smoking could be a contributory cause of cancer of the lung. I am conscious of the risk that anything we say on this matter might appear to be prejudiced. I can assure you, however, that we have been following very closely the research on this subject. We have a very real sense of the need to view this matter objectively, and it is in that spirit that I would state quite categorically that the available evidence is far from conclusive and by no means constitutes proof that tobacco can be a contributory cause of this disease. It is said that there is a statistical correlation; but there is, in fact, a considerable weight of statistical evidence against the validity of the accusations that are made against tobacco in this connection. Moreover, possible correlatives other than smoking have been suggested by several medical authorities. It has never been our policy to make exaggerated claims for the smoking habit, or to say that it confers on those who indulge in it benefits other than the pleasure and peace of mind it may bring. Equally, however, we can assert that in our manufacture we do everything possible to maintain the highest standards of purity and quality in our products. We shall, of course, continue to keep in the closest touch with all the investigations that are going on, and if it should ever be proved that there exists something harmful in tobacco, even in the minutest quantities, which could conceivably make smoking one of the causes of this disease, we should, I hope, be the first to take steps to eliminate it.'

19. Sir Harold Himsworth recorded a discussion on 7 April 1953 with Professor Alexander Haddow, one of those suggested by Green, noting that Haddow, approached by Partridge, had told him that he found Doll and Hill's case strong and had 'warned [Partridge] off undertaking biological experiments' but had said that 'the tobacco people either had or could easily get' information about the chemical composition of smoke and tars.

20. BMJ 1953; i: 1362-3, 14 February 1953.

21. PRO file MH 55.1011

22. Professor M J Kendall (London School of Economics), Dr W P D Logan (Central Statistical Office) and Dr P L McKinlay (Superintendent of Statistics at the Scottish General Registry Office).

23. PRO file MH 55.1011

24. PRO file MH 55.1011. The Ministry attitude can be contrasted with the advice from a 'recent' editorial in the *British Medical Journal* quoted by Dr Goodman in a brief attached to the minute (quoted below) that went to the Minister: 'all we can do is show that the probability of a causative connection between an agent and disease is so great that we are bound to take what preventive action we can, accepting the theory as though the proof was absolute until further research leads to some modification.' (I have not been able to identify this editorial.)

25. The final version of the last paragraph was as follows (the changes from the Ministry version are italicised): 'Although no *immediate* dramatic fall in death-rates could be expected if smoking ceased, since the development of lung cancer may be the result of factors operating over many years, *and although no reliable quantitative estimates can be made of the effect of smoking on the incidence of cancer of the lung,* it is desirable that young people should be warned of the risks apparently attendant on excessive smoking. *It would appear that the risk increases with the amount smoked, particularly of cigarettes.*' - PRO file MH 133.453.

26. Minute, quoted below, by J E Pater, Undersecretary, 19 January 1954, which eventually went to the Minister - PRO file MH 55.1011.

27. Sir George Godber writes: 'Horace Joules enlivened the CHSC and SMAC but his political background meant that he was dropped fairly soon. If he had not rebelled we might never have got them moving.' (Personal communication, 19 January 1998)

28. PRO file MH 133.450

29. PRO files MH 55.1011, MH 133.453

30. PRO file FD 1.2009

31. A Board of Trade file opened in 1955 records that Sir Alexander Maxwell, a tobacco leaf merchant, was appointed Tobacco Controller in 1940 to deal with wartime shortages. He had two committees to advise him - the Tobacco

Manufacturers Advisory Committee and the Tobacco Distributors Advisory Committee. After the war, he became unpaid Tobacco Adviser to the Board of Trade while continuing with his own business. The TDAC had last met in 1949, but the TMAC, commonly known as the Tobacco Advisory Committee, was still meeting ten times a year on Board of Trade premises and with Board of Trade servicing. However, it was operating purely as a manufacturers' association: the Board of Trade (the file records) rarely had need of advice and never asked the Committee for it. Maxwell, moreover, was inclined to use his position to obtain or seek to obtain commercially confidential information lodged with the Board of Trade by tobacco companies, which he was not above making use of for his own ends and revealing to others, again to the Board of Trade's embarrassment. The Board of Trade decided to wind up the two committees but did not succeed in doing so until Maxwell retired three years later - PRO file BT 258.284.

32. Personal communication, 19 January 1998. Given the high prevalence of smoking at the time, especially by men, most of the officials dealing with the subject were inevitably smokers.

33. H.A.(54)9, 26 January 1954 - PRO file CAB 134.916

34. This reference is to the notorious 'Frank Statement' published in 448 US newspapers, on and shortly after 4 January 1954 which announced the establishment of the Tobacco Industry Research Council (later the Council for Tobacco Research). It is now on record that this was from the start no more than a public relations move, the creation of the PR company Hill & Knowlton (see, for example, pp 39-40 of Glantz, Slade, Bero, Hanauer and Barnes, *The Cigarette Papers*, University of California Press, 1996, quoting internal tobacco industry documents). The British industry's offer seems to have been less cynical, since the MRC's research, unlike the CTR's, would be genuinely independent.

35. Joules had been in the summer of 1951 chairman of a scientific delegation to Russia from the Society for Cultural Relations with the USSR and praised his hosts for already then publicising the link between smoking and lung cancer whereas by contrast 'in this country . . . he had had little success in publicizing this fact' - *The Times*, 15 August 1951.

36. Brief, 1 February 1954, by Sir Harold Himsworth for the Lord President of the Council - PRO file CAB 124.1670. This paper is further quoted below.

37. The Lord President derives his title from his role in the Privy Council, of which the MRC is technically a committee.

38. Minute, 8 February 1954, from Sir Harold Himsworth to the Lord President of the Council - PRO file CAB 124.1670.

39. PRO file CAB 124.1670

40. PRO file CAB 124.1670

41.   C.(54)47 - PRO file CAB 129.65

42.   GEN 456/2 - PRO file CAB 130.100

43.   C.(54)51 - PRO file CAB 129.66

44.   C.C.(54) 8th - PRO file CAB 128.27

45.   Calling themselves 'a group of leading tobacco manufacturers in the United Kingdom', they listed themselves as Ardath Tobacco Co Ltd, British-American Tobacco Co Ltd, Carreras Ltd, George Dobie & Son Ltd, Gallaher Ltd, Imperial Tobacco Co. (of Great Britain & Ireland) Ltd, Godfrey Phillips Ltd and J Wix & Sons Ltd - PRO file MH 55.1011.

2

1954-57: Neutralising the MRC Findings

The public did not entirely ignore the risks of smoking: many of them wrote to the Minister of Health and a file in the Public Record Office[1] preserves some of their theories and proposals. One correspondent claimed that lung cancer was caused by the sulphur in matches, another blamed petrol lighters, and a former TB nurse blamed the Russians. A State Registered Nurse blamed stray contaminants on the fingers of smokers, and other writers pointed to causes quite removed from smoking: exhaust fumes, salt-petre in artificial fertiliser, dust from rubber tyres, chlorinated water supplies or contamination from wild rabbits. A woman enclosed the fading and torn manuscript of her grandmother's remedy for cancer, which involved boiling a poultice of figs in milk, and an eighty-one-year-old claimed that dog-ends were being sold back to the manufacturers for re-use as an economy measure.

Amid the paranoid suggestions of far-reaching plots 'to destroy our health and security, as I have for 15 years on end warned H M Ministers of State at risk of being murdered for doing so' and those out for gain ('I believe I know the answer and would let you know by <u>return</u> of post if you are interested, providing I am not to be forgot when proved') there are sensible letters also: a correspondent noted that cigarettes were now smoked down to a very short butt owing to the shortage of tobacco; another suggested experiments on monkeys, and a Miss Marjorie Marrian - not the only one to point to the potential risks to non-smokers - proposed studying lung cancer in non-smokers working in smoky areas such as usherettes in cinemas. One person complained to the Minister of the failure of the *Daily Telegraph* to publish anti- as well as pro-smoking letters.

Tom Hurst - who went on to long years of service to the National Society of Non-Smokers[2] and was the originator of the UK's No Smoking Day campaign - wrote to the Minister that he and his wife proposed to initiate a campaign to persuade smokers to quit smoking and asked: 'Would you, Sir, be prepared to support such a campaign, subject to the details being settled by your department?' The reply stated that 'the Minister feels he is unable to support campaigns which might mislead the public into assuming that a causal relationship between tobacco smoking and cancer had been definitely proved.' Another letter was from the president of the Non-Smoking Publicity Society, who sought withdrawal of tobacco advertising on public transport.

This wish to control tobacco advertising was soon echoed in Parliament, where the Bill to establish commercial television was being discussed. On 31 May, Dr Barnet Stross, Labour MP for Stoke on Trent Central, moved an amendment to ban tobacco advertising from the new channel, and the Home Secretary, David Maxwell Fyfe, undertook to consult his colleagues on the point. When the General Post Office, responsible for broadcasting, wrote accordingly to the Ministry of Health, M R P Gregson, an Assistant Secretary, suggested to Dr Goodman: 'I think it would be quite wrong to ban tobacco advertisements on commercial television. Why pick on tobacco - what about alcohol?' Goodman responded: 'I entirely agree. If and when (a) a causal association is proved (b) public opinion accepts that all tobacco advertising might be immoral, a ban might be considered. We are very far from either at present.'

Gregson therefore replied to the GPO, in terms agreed by the Minister, that 'any hasty and ill-considered ban such as that suggested would mislead the public into assuming that a causal relationship between tobacco smoking and cancer has been definitely and unequivocally proved.' He referred to the research being undertaken and the 'large sum of money' provided by the industry for such research. 'In view of this, it would in the Minister's view, be wrong to take any step such as that suggested.' The next day the Permanent Secretary's private office notified the Chief Medical Officer and Mr Gregson that 'Mr Partridge, of the Imperial Tobacco Company, is coming to see the [Permanent] Secretary on Wednesday, 23rd June', and Partridge himself wrote to Sir John Hawton a few days later to say that the purpose of the visit was to talk about the Television Bill debate. Sir John minuted after the meeting: 'I replied to him broadly in the sense of the letter sent by Mr Gregson to the Post Office on the 16th June and he seemed perfectly satisfied and said that that was what he expected.'[3]

This complacent attitude in the Ministry of Health is brilliantly illuminated when at just this time the *British Medical Journal* published the first report from Richard Doll and Austin Bradford Hill on their study of British doctors - a report brought forward owing to the unexpected strength of the case it made against smoking.[4] The event passes without notice. Not even a press cutting is filed.[5] The Ministry maintained in public that it awaited further research: in fact it ignored research and was moved to action only by external pressure.

The research nevertheless continued.[6] The MRC held a conference in June 1954 and set up two working committees - one chemical, one biological - to oversee research on 'the chemistry of tobacco smoke in relation to carcinogenesis'. These committees met - sometimes together - roughly once a year and reviewed technical research papers. In 1954 and again in 1956 visits were paid to the Imperial Tobacco research laboratory in Bristol. Further papers were published by Doll and Hill and by other researchers, but the story was now one of politics, not of science.

Horace Joules, dropped from the Standing Advisory Committee (Cancer and Radiotherapy), was still a member of the Standing Medical Advisory Committee (SMAC) and he persuaded it on 8 March 1955 that although the former committee covered 'the nature of the connection' it was within the SMAC's remit to consider publicity. He urged that 'it was vital that the public should be reminded constantly of the known facts and of the risks involved in heavy smoking.' He succeeded, and the SMAC advised the Minister that it was 'desirable that appropriate action should be taken constantly to inform the public of the known connection between smoking and cancer of the lung and of the risks involved in heavy smoking'.

Once more the Ministry of Health had to face the problem. R L Briggs, a principal in the Ministry, consulted Dr Goodman and then wrote to Gregson:

> the Minister could agree to make a further announcement . . . but not at this stage to keep up a steady barrage of propaganda as [SMAC] want. Apart from the uncertainty which still remains about the culpability of tobacco - though we have admitted that it seems to have some measure of culpability - no doubt the Chancellor of the Exchequer would be interested!

The Ministry produced a paper for the Central Health Services Council (through which the SMAC's advice had to be routed) in which the history of the SAC(CR)'s consideration of the matter was related, including the report of the Government Actuary's committee and the Minister's announcement the previous year. It recalled the SAC(CR)'s advice in 1949 against cancer education of the general public. The CHSC had agreed that it was wrong 'to make the public cancer-conscious by fear', but had left the door open for local authorities to undertake publicity. In 1952, the SAC(CR) had recognised the value of 'reducing the delay between the onset of symptoms and consultation of the general practitioner' and had positively advised that local authorities and voluntary bodies undertake cancer education: the Minister had accordingly issued a circular to local health authorities in August 1953.[7]

The CHSC did not meet until October 1955 and then they rejected the SMAC's advice. It would be 'wise' to await the outcome of research, including that financed by the 'considerable sum' provided by the tobacco companies. Besides, 'it was understood that further research by the Medical Research Council was throwing some doubt on the causal connection between smoking and cancer of the lung.' It is not clear who provided this misinformation, but it doubtless encouraged Imperial Tobacco's secretary, Partridge, who visited the Ministry of Health Permanent Secretary, Sir John Hawton, shortly afterwards to find out what had happened.[8] (These visits and telephone calls were almost routine: he had called previously in July - 'He wanted to know whether there were any developments since the M[inister]'s answer [to a Parliamentary Question] in the House on the 27th June.' - and in March 1956 we find him consulting Sir John on the wording of Imperial Tobacco's annual report. The following month he sought help with a plan - later dropped - for Dr Clarence Cook Little, scientific director of the US Tobacco Industry Research Council (later known as the Council for Tobacco Research), to meet 'leading medical correspondents' during a visit to the UK.)

The subject would not go away. In March 1956, the Minister of Health, now Robin Turton, in an exchange in the House of Commons, stated, presumably without realising the implications: 'There is a causal connection between smoking and lung cancer. That we know.' The next day Partridge was on the phone to Sir John to protest, and a few days later the Treasury's Second Secretary, Sir Herbert Brittain, wrote to express concern that the Minister's remarks went beyond Iain Macleod's 1954 statement, which had conceded only the 'presumption of a causal connection': 'We have a close interest in the public discussion of this subject [lung cancer] and its association in such discussions with smoking, because of the very considerable revenue (£660 millions) which we derive from tobacco duties.' Sir John hastened to reassure them: there was no change of policy: the Minister's words were 'an oral slip'.[9]

But by then the Central Health Services Council had bent to the reiterated will of the SMAC and transmitted to the Minister its advice in favour of constant publicity 'as a matter of urgency'. The minutes of their meeting on 13 March record their conclusions:

> (a)   Propaganda on this subject was not analogous to the ordinary type of cancer education which was aimed primarily at the early detection of cancers: it was rather a piece of purely preventive medicine.

(b)   Propaganda on smoking and lung cancer was becoming urgent. The public were constantly exposed to propaganda in favour of smoking and efforts to inform them of its connection with cancer had so far had little success.

(c)   There was already sufficient evidence of a causal connection . . . to justify a centrally directed propaganda campaign, for example through schools and general practitioners.

Further, it was difficult to define 'excessive' - there was a straight-line correlation between the number of cigarettes smoked and the risk of lung cancer, and the risk even for heavy smokers was reduced if they stopped smoking.[10]

The Minister was back in the firing line. He immediately came under pressure in the House of Commons[11] to say what he was going to do. The Chancellor - now Harold Macmillan - was quick to enter his *caveat*:

Dear Robin

The effect of smoking on the incidence of lung cancer is very much back in the news. I gather that you have decided that you will have to make some statement on the subject, and that you have it in mind to refer this in draft to the Home Affairs Committee.

In view of the enormous yield of the tobacco duty, the subject is one in which the Exchequer is very much involved. I would therefore like to have a talk with you about your statement before it is considered by the Home Affairs Committee. Our Private Secretaries can fix a time. - Harold Macmillan

Turton replied reassuringly[12], and it was not until 11 April that he put a paper to the Home Affairs committee of the Cabinet.[13] It summarised the evidence on smoking and health and quoted the chairman of the MRC's committee on the subject, Professor Alexander Haddow. He had pointed to the known potent carcinogen 3:4-benzpyrene as a likely agent in causing lung cancer but admitted that the chemical work, owing to 'natural experimental and technical difficulties', was inconclusive. However:

The fact that a causal agent has not yet been recognised should, in my opinion, not be allowed to confuse the main issue, namely, that there is a statistical association between cigarette smoking and the incidence of lung cancer which (again in my opinion) is so massive as to be incontrovertible; and the simplest explanation of which is that there is a causal connection between the two.

Turton, however, stated that the evidence, however 'incontrovertible', was 'not conclusive enough to justify the kind of national propaganda campaign which my advisory bodies urge' and proposed only to answer a Parliamentary Question with a 'progress report' on the research, in which he would say that although progress was being made, there was 'not yet any scientifically conclusive proof', so that he felt unable to go further than making the (briefly summarised) facts known.[14] Moreover, his statement should not (he proposed) come until after the impending Budget, and he had persuaded an MP with a question on the House of Commons order paper that it should be postponed.

The Lord President, Lord Salisbury, was briefed on Turton's paper by the MRC and his own office.[15] H B Lewin, a principal in his office, complained of the excessive caution of the proposed statement ('so carefully worded' with 'so many qualifications') which resulted in the Minister in effect reneging on Iain Macleod's 1954 statement that it was desirable that young people be warned of the risks of excessive smoking. Landsborough Thomson, now Sir Arthur, in a restrained minute, nevertheless made it clear that the Minister of Health was understating his case. His Council's 'own assessment of the degree of proof already attained' would 'almost certainly' be 'substantially higher . . . [A]bsolute scientific proof of causation . . . is always difficult to achieve' but already in this case 'the evidence is stronger than that which, in comparable matters, is commonly taken as a basis for definite action' - a formulation that was to reappear, and disappear, the following year.

The Cabinet Home Affairs committee met on 13 April with R A Butler in the chair.[16] Lord Salisbury dutifully reported that the MRC would have preferred a stronger statement. 'The evidence linking cancer of the lung and smoking had increased notably since 1954, and was now stronger than would normally be regarded as justifying action.' In discussion, the need 'to retain a sense of proportion and to avoid creating anything resembling panic' was set against the fact that lung cancer was 'dreaded' and that there was 'little doubt' that proof of the causal connection 'would be obtained, and probably fairly soon'. The Chancellor confirmed that it would be 'most inconvenient' to have the statement before the Budget, and the proposed statement was approved subject to endorsement by the full Cabinet.

The paper to the Cabinet repeated the main points put to the Home Affairs committee. At the Cabinet meeting on 19 April, Turton said that

> The statement which he proposed to make was restrained rather than alarmist. It would not satisfy those who felt that the situation demanded a general propaganda campaign, in the schools and elsewhere, against smoking. He considered, however, that this would not be justified in the absence of direct scientific proof of a causal connection between smoking and lung cancer.

But he did not get things all his own way:

> The Prime Minister [Sir Anthony Eden] said that, in his view, the time had come when the Government should determine their attitude to

this problem and decide whether or not they should take a definite line on it. He proposed that a small Committee of Ministers should go more fully into the problem and submit their views and recommendations to the Cabinet.

This was agreed[17], and the Committee was set up with R A Butler, the Lord Privy Seal, in the chair, and with Lord Salisbury (Lord President of the Council), James Stuart (Secretary of State for Scotland), Harold Macmillan (Chancellor of the Exchequer) and Robin Turton (Minister of Health) as members. Its terms of reference were

> To recommend what policy the Government should adopt in the light of the statistical evidence which appears to establish a relationship between smoking and cancer of the lung, and to report to the Cabinet.

The Committee - known as GEN 524[18] - met a week later to consider a revised and rather inept draft Parliamentary Answer in which Robin Turton tried to take account of points made at the Cabinet meeting: 'The extent of the problem should not be exaggerated . . . in 1954, for men aged 45-74, out of every thousand deaths eight were from motor vehicle accidents, eighty-five were from cancer of the lung and seventy-seven were from bronchitis' - the contribution of smoking to bronchitis had not yet been highlighted. However, it included the information that 'by giving up smoking the risk can be materially reduced' and the statements that the Government believed the time had come to draw the facts to public attention and that 'more should be done to foster research towards developing a cigarette which is free from carcinogenic substances'.

The Committee, however, decided that the statement should minimise any 'expression of opinion or concern' by the Government. The statistical comparisons should substitute strokes and apoplexies (112 deaths per 1000) for road accidents; the advice about giving up smoking was 'unnecessary', as was the reference to developing a carcinogen-free cigarette.

Turton produced a redraft. It quoted the MRC committee chairman as saying that the risk of lung cancer among heavy smokers was twenty times that in non-smokers and said that the Government considered that 'the public should be kept informed of all relevant information as and when it becomes available'. This version was put to the Cabinet in a paper by Butler which stated the extent to which the Government should accept responsibility in some detail:

> Any statement on this subject should not involve the Government too deeply in responsibility for dealing with the possible consequences of excessive smoking. From the point of view of social hygiene, cancer of the lung is not a disease like tuberculosis; nor should the Government assume too lightly the odium of advising the general

> public on their personal tastes and habits where the evidence of harm which may result is not conclusive.

> . . . the Minister's statement should, as far as possible, rest, without comment, upon the views of the medical experts, and it should aim to hold the balance evenly between unnecessarily alarming public opinion, and dismissing the whole question as unimportant. A statement falling between these two extremes would be as clear as can be expected in the present state of our knowledge, and should also take care of the substantial Treasury interest involved.

The statement ought also to anticipate the expected new report from Doll and Bradford Hill and 'do so with the minimum of ostentation, i.e., preferably by way of an ordinary Parliamentary Question.'

The Cabinet approved this version with minor amendments[19] and the same day Turton arranged to see Sir Alexander Maxwell 'as Chairman of the Tobacco Advisory Committee of the Board of Trade' - presumably to inform him of the terms of the statement, although there is no minute of the meeting on the file.

The result was that, when finally on 7 May Turton delivered the agreed answer in the Commons (reproduced in the Appendix), with the addition in answer to a supplementary question that 'In my view, in the present stage of our knowledge, a national publicity campaign would not be appropriate', the tobacco companies were able simultaneously to issue a statement to the press emphasising that the evidence was 'conflicting and very incomplete' with a great deal more research needed before firm conclusions could be drawn. They stressed that the 'suggestion that smoking may be a contributory cause of lung cancer continues to be based mainly on certain statistical enquiries' which could 'never constitute proof of a cause and effect relationship'. They made the most of what anomalies they could find, claimed that 'tobacco is a great boon to many millions of people in this country and throughout the world', and anticipated later industry lines of enquiry by suggesting that 'the benefits, psychological and physiological, it may confer are not yet fully understood and might well be a subject of scientific investigation'. They allowed that an excess of anything was harmful - but what was excess? - and concluded by stressing the need for the research that their £250,000 was funding.[20]

After such a masterly performance, the companies must have been disappointed that *The Times* the next day was critical of Robin Turton, saying that his statement had 'added nothing to public knowledge and subtracted nothing from public anxiety'. It picked on 'ministerial fatuities' and called for an end to 'platitudinizing', giving a long list of discerning questions that needed answers. While 'it is foolish to press a science for more certainty than it is capable of giving' nevertheless 'the time has come for his Ministry to summarize the ascertained facts, put them into plain language and publish them in a cheap and arresting format'. However, the industry's disappointment at such criticism must have been as nothing compared with the disillusion of Horace Joules and his allies whose efforts over five years had been rewarded so meagrely.[21]

The tobacco companies now consolidated their position by formalising the group that had provided the £250,000 as the Tobacco Manufacturers' Standing Committee (known later as the Tobacco Research Council). It was already in action - complaining about a Ministry of Education handbook that included the MRC's claim that the risk of lung cancer for heavy smokers was 20 times that for non-smokers: the calculation was Bradford Hill's but it had not been scientifically published - before its formation was announced in a statement issued on 3 August. Maxwell was its chairman, and Sir Alfred Egerton FRS and Sir Ronald Fisher FRS had 'consented to act as Scientific Consultants to the Committee'. Egerton had been Professor of Chemical Technology at Imperial College from 1936 to 1952 and Secretary of the Royal Society for ten years to 1948; Fisher had been since 1943 the Arthur Balfour Professor of Genetics at Cambridge and was a past President of the Royal Statistical Society. Fisher, in particular, was a valuable ally to the industry.[22]

Lord Salisbury, however, had privately but formally asked the MRC in May 'to review the evidence . . . and to prepare a statement of their considered assessment of the significance of the present knowledge'.[23] The resulting Ministerial statement did not come until June 1957, and for the intervening year the Government merely brushed the issue aside. Numbers of questions were asked in Parliament pressing for publicity. The answers followed the same line: for example, in November 1956 Robin Turton claimed that the recently published second report from Doll and Hill[24] merely 'confirms the statistical association . . . about which I made a statement in the House on 7th May . . . I do not consider that a [national] campaign [of information] such as the Hon. Member . . . suggests would be at present appropriate.'

The SMAC in December repeated its advice on the basis of Doll and Hill's new report that the Minister should 'constantly . . . inform the public' of the risks and the CHSC agreed - but to no avail. The Ministry files contain a report of a conference in January 1957 of the Central Council for Health Education - a joint body of the local authorities - at which Dr John Burton, its Medical Director, 'spoke of the contradictory attitudes towards smoking and cancer; the Minister refusing to do any anti-smoking publicity; the subsidy for the tobacco for troops and old age pensioners; doctors' personal attitude to smoking and their shrugging off their failure to stop by attributing it to "lack of will power".'

In March 1957, Marcus Lipton, Labour MP for Brixton, who had been the principal author of recent Parliamentary Questions, obtained an adjournment debate on the subject.[25] He referred to the prevalence of smoking

- two in every three men and two in every five women were smokers, and 2s 6d (12.5p) in every pound spent in the shops went on tobacco - and complained of the Government's 'old gramophone record' of waiting for better information: 'The Government are very actively concerned in doing nothing at all'. He condemned as 'probably the most disgusting and immoral thing that any Minister of the Crown has ever said' a remark by the Chancellor of the Exchequer, Peter Thorneycroft, that 'We at the Treasury do not want too many people to stop smoking' and quoted Dr Horace Joules and Dr J G Scadding, also a member of SMAC and the leading chest physician of the day, to reinforce his call for Government publicity to counteract the £2¼ million annual press and television advertising for tobacco.

He was immediately accused of 'scoring cheap points' by Richard Fort, the Conservative MP for Clitheroe and a lay member of the Medical Research Council, who claimed that even Professor Bradford Hill thought further statistical analysis necessary, to which should be added animal research and work on air pollution. Shedding crocodile tears for the 'really tragic increasing rate of lung cancer' he deplored Marcus Lipton's speech as 'merely rais[ing] a smokescreen rather than throw[ing] clarity on this difficult problem'. This was an apt prelude to the reply to the debate by J K Vaughan-Morgan, the Parliamentary Secretary at the Ministry of Health, who rehearsed history at length and deplored 'unnecessary sensationalism' and 'hasty' conclusions. A week later a written answer revealed that the death rate from lung cancer had risen from 279 per million in 1950 to 389 in 1955.[26]

By then the Medical Research Council had produced its draft statement on smoking and lung cancer.[27]

> So far, no adequate explanation for the large increase in the mortality rates from lung cancer has been advanced save that smoking is indeed a principal factor in the causation of the disease. Absolute scientific proof of causation, as distinct from circumstantial evidence, is always difficult to achieve; it might in this instance never be achieved, there being no obvious method of devising a crucial experiment in man.

The draft discounted the likely results of the Council's own chemical and biological research and proceeded:

> In scientific work, as in the practical affairs of everyday life, conclusions have often to be founded on the most reasonable and probable explanation of the observed facts. The evidence of a causal relationship between smoking and lung cancer, which is now extensive and very detailed, follows the classic pattern upon which many advances in the past have been made in preventive medicine. The recognition of the risk of cancer run by chimney sweeps and tar workers, for example, came many years before the responsible carcinogenic agents were isolated, and it was action based upon the

purely statistical and epidemiological investigations of Dr Snow which
stamped out cholera epidemics in this country seventeen years before
the infecting organism was first seen under the microscope . . .

After reviewing possible causes of the continuing rise in lung cancer
deaths and its strong links to tobacco smoking, the statement attributed a
'relatively small number' to 'specific industrial hazards' and 'an unknown
proportion, probably not exceeding 20%' to atmospheric pollution. The
evidence, however, pointed to smoking being responsible for 'a major part of
the increase', and the 'most reasonable interpretation' was that this was a
matter of 'direct cause and effect'. The final conclusions were:

(6)   Conclusive proof is unlikely to be obtained unless it becomes
        possible to study the effects of a reduction of smoking on a
        mass scale.

(7)   The evidence now available is stronger than that which, in
        comparable matters, is commonly taken as the basis for
        definite action.

At the Ministry of Health Dr Goodman was characteristically
unimpressed. 'It is a re-appraisal, not the presentation of new evidence, and
the M.R.C. position has advanced primarily because of the failure to produce
any rebutting evidence. . .' He criticised the use of the word 'direct' in 'direct
cause and effect'.

In my view, a major source of the smoking habit is during compulsory
service in the Services, when cigarettes are cheaply and easily available
and there is nothing much else to do but smoke. There is no doubt
that smoking is diminishing among the educated classes but this has
not yet affected consumption figures but the example of these classes
will eventually have an effect. Apart from education, a restrictive
increase in taxation on tobacco would not I think greatly diminish
revenue because the addicts would continue but might reduce the
numbers acquiring the habit.[28]

An Assistant Secretary, R W Bavin, after consultation with Dr
Goodman, wrote to the Undersecretary, J E Pater, on 1 April: 'The Chancellor
of the Exchequer would no doubt strongly oppose publication, and the
tobacco companies would do all they could to rebut it if it was publicised' but
conceded that there was little possibility of avoiding publication. As to further
action, some restrictions on smoking in public places might be possible but
'exposure to other people's smoke is not thought to be of great importance'
and the effect on smokers' consumption would be insignificant 'as I know
from personal experience in North America where such restrictions are, of
course, in force.' Propaganda would be difficult 'without a definite, clear-cut,
easily understandable theme' which the MRC statement did not provide, as

1. . . . we do not know how smoking causes lung cancer and

2. . . . we cannot say that it is the only cause.

How, he asked, could a propaganda campaign be conducted? There was little alternative but to work through the local health authorities, but while they were routinely in touch with mothers and young children - the usual focus for health education - they had much less contact with men. 'The influence which might be exerted on the effectiveness of such a campaign by the opposition of the tobacco companies would also have to be considered; and of course, it would be necessary to carry the Treasury and, indeed, the Cabinet . . .' He then ventured the unorthodox opinion that perhaps 'the Government should itself somehow communicate with the public direct' rather than rely on press and radio to report statements in Parliament - presumably 'some sort of leaflet' might be produced for sale or free distribution.[29]

Sir John Charles, the Chief Medical Officer, was less complacent than his subordinate Dr Goodman: he wrote to the Deputy Secretary, Dame Enid Russell-Smith:

The new MRC statement is much more positive than anything that has come from them hitherto. It does not reflect new knowledge so much as a more intensely held conviction that excessive cigarette smoking causes a considerable number of avoidable deaths. It is clear also that short of some unexpected discovery on the chemical side, they do not expect to have any more convincing evidence than they have at present . . . [As to] practical repercussions . . . I am attracted by [Mr Bavin's] suggestion of some sort of pamphlet . . . though it would presumably stimulate a counterblast by the tobacco interests.

Dame Enid was not attracted by the idea of a pamphlet: in her memorandum to the Permanent Secretary she saw any publicity as being handled by the local health authorities, and if they wanted a 'popular pamphlet for the man in the street' it would be prepared by the Central Council for Health Education 'subject of course to our approval . . .':

If this kind of pattern were followed, direct Government action would be kept to a minimum, effort would be dispersed, and it would be much more difficult for the Tobacco Companies to organise counter-action.[30]

On 10 April Sir Harold Himsworth, the Secretary of the MRC, forwarded a revised version of their statement to their Minister, the Lord President, now Lord Home, observing that it was 'suitable for publication if that is desired'. The revision attributed up to 30% (rather than 20%) of lung cancer deaths to atmospheric pollution, compressed into a single paragraph the two quoted on page 46 and omitted conclusion (6) (as quoted above) altogether.[31]

One of his staff minuted to Lord Home that he would no doubt wish to consult Sir Harold Himsworth about the report and

> You may like particularly to ask Sir H. Himsworth what force to attach to the last paragraph 6. of the conclusions of the memorandum

- that is, after the omission of the original conclusion (6), the conclusion quoted above as (7): 'The evidence now available is stronger than that which, in comparable matters, is commonly taken as the basis for definite action.'

This troublesome pointer to the need for Government action was obviously giving cause for concern. The consultations that ensued are not evident on any of the files, but by 23 April, when Lord Home put a paper to the relevant Cabinet committee[32], he felt able to say that the MRC considered their statement suitable for publication 'apart from Conclusion 6'.[33] At an 'office talk' on 1 May the Minister of Health, now Dennis Vosper, concluded

> it would be quite impossible to resist publication of the M.R.C. statement. It would, however, be desirable if Conclusion (6) were omitted, particularly if the Government were not at the same time announcing that they were going to take action on the statement. The only possible danger was that the existence of a Conclusion which has been suppressed might possibly leak out.[34]

The Cabinet committee met on 7 May, with R A Butler in the chair.[35] Lord Home, who had previously warned his colleagues that the MRC were about to publish in their annual report the statement that

> So far no adequate explanation of all this statistical evidence has been advanced except that of direct cause and effect - that smoking is, indeed, a principal factor in the causation of the disease [i.e., lung cancer][36]

now proposed that the Government publish the MRC statement simultaneously with the Council's annual report.

Dennis Vosper urged the exclusion of conclusion (6) but then turned to matters of cost. If the Central Council for Health Education were required to undertake a publicity campaign, they 'would certainly ask for some financial support'. Central funding of the CCHE had recently been ended, leaving it dependent on the local authorities, and Ministers were reluctant to reverse that policy. Dr Charles Hill pointed out, however, that even £10,000 for leaflets would be 'a considerable proportion of the total income of the CCHE. But this might only be the beginning, since a campaign with pamphlets alone would be ineffective and the Council would no doubt wish to use all the modern media, including television, with a consequent increase in expenditure.'[37]

Peter Thorneycroft, the Chancellor of the Exchequer, warned that 'any campaign with Government support, even if carried out indirectly through the

CCHE, would need the most careful consideration; for once this course was embarked on it would be difficult to resist the pressure for an intensive propaganda campaign which would distort the proper functions of the Council' and lead to pressure to renew its grant. Besides,

> The Committee were already aware of the enormous contribution to the Exchequer from tobacco duties and the serious effect on the Commonwealth, in particular on Rhodesia, that a campaign against smoking would have.

The Committee noted that the tobacco companies 'would be certain to embark on a powerful campaign of publicity in opposition to the CCHE. They should, however, be given advance warning of the Government's intention to publish the MRC's findings, and the question of the need for further research should be discussed with them as well as with the MRC.' Meantime Lord Home, wearing his other hat as Commonwealth Secretary, would enquire what other Governments were doing[38] and the Minister of Health would draft a statement.

The process of drafting took three weeks. The CCHE were not informed 'as this would set rumours flying'[39]. The Ministry of Education commented on an early draft:

> It is not quite accurate to say that the Handbook included advice on how best to discourage smoking by children. The emphasis in the Handbook was on self-control or restraint and it did not say in terms that children should be advised not to smoke.[40]

The Ministry of Health's Public Relations and Principal Press Officer, S A Heald, suggested that the Minister's Parliamentary statement be accompanied by a lobby conference, a press conference, a recorded statement for radio, a television interview and so on and be followed up with leaflets, a poster and a filmstrip and that an approach should possibly be made to the armed forces medical services. Discouraged by Dame Enid Russell-Smith and Sir John Hawton from anything beyond a lobby conference and a circular to local authorities, Dennis Vosper recorded: 'I would have thought that we shall need to take all action suggested by Mr Heald in connection with my statement but little or nothing of the action suggested for follow-up publicity. This is for the C.C.H.E.' In keeping with this policy of a burst of self-publicity without effective follow-through, a sentence in the draft Ministerial statement put to the Minister's private secretary on 27 May saying that 'The Government . . . will not hesitate to stimulate further action if, in their view, this appears to be advisable' disappeared from the version submitted to the Cabinet committee on 31 May.[41]

The paper proposed that a Ministerial statement be made after the Whitsun recess simultaneously with the publication of the MRC's annual report and 'special report' on lung cancer (from which 'they . . . propose to delete the last conclusion (No. 6)'). The draft Ministerial statement, which had been agreed with the MRC and the Scottish Office but not with the Treasury[42], said that the MRC now advised that 'a major part' of the increase in lung cancer was 'caused by smoking tobacco, particularly in the form of cigarettes'.

> The Government feel that it is their duty to ensure that this latest and
> most authoritative opinion is brought effectively to public notice

but proposed to do so only by circulars to local education and health authorities. The Councils for Health Education in England and Scotland would assist local health authorities, but not - as the covering paper to the Committee made clear - act independently: by charging for their leaflets they should be required to cover their costs.

The proposed statement continued:

> Once the risks are known everyone who smokes will have to measure
> them and make up his own mind. People have a duty to themselves,
> and to the community which bears so much of the burden of illness;
> perhaps, above all, if they are parents, they have a duty to their
> children. In a matter so personal they must be relied upon as
> responsible citizens to act as they think best.

It concluded with two paragraphs about the continuing programme of research, complete with acknowledgement of the 'generous benefaction made in 1954 by a leading group of Tobacco Manufacturers'.

The draft was discussed by the Cabinet committee on 3 June. The paragraph quoted above on personal responsibility was considered

> too emotional. A bare statement of facts which did not endeavour to
> point a moral would have a greater psychological impact. The
> Government should not seek to intrude into the sphere of an
> individual's personal responsibility. It was, however, important to
> stress this element of personal choice since direct Government action
> was excluded.

The next day a revised version of the statement was put to the Cabinet itself[43]. The offending paragraph was reduced to two lines:

> Once the risks are known everyone who smokes will have to measure
> them and make up his or her own mind, and must be relied upon as
> a responsible person to act as seems best.

The Cabinet met on 6 June with Harold Macmillan, now Prime Minister, in the chair. They agreed two further amendments to the draft:

(a)   The Government should not admit a 'duty' to warn the public
        of the connection between smoking and lung cancer. This

disease could be differentiated from those, such as tuberculosis and poliomyelitis, which were infectious or contagious;

(b)   The opening sentence of the statement should be amended to indicate that the risk of lung cancer was greatest in connection with heavy smoking of cigarettes.

As a result the final version of the statement attributed the increase in lung cancer to 'smoking tobacco, particularly heavy cigarette smoking' and had the Government feeling it 'right' to ensure that what it now called 'this latest authoritative opinion' (rather than 'latest and most authoritative') was brought to public notice.

Before the statement was made there was further interaction with the tobacco industry. Partly this concerned the timing of publication of the first annual report of the Tobacco Manufacturers Standing Committee (TMSC)[44]. More significantly, on 30 May the Minister of Health's private office was warned - probably by Heald - that

The Lord President's Office propose to show the draft Parliamentary statement before it is made to representatives of the tobacco companies financing the research. I have emphasised that on our experience this, if it is done, ought to take place on the same day as the statement is made.

Nevertheless, it would seem that the consultation took place in time for the TMSC to produce a considered response to the MRC report on the same day it was published and the Ministerial statement was made - 27 June. The TMSC statement sought to reassure smokers:

At this stage any conclusions are a matter of opinion. The Medical Research Council have expressed one view. Other authorities in the scientific fields concerned have expressed different views . . .

The MRC had produced no new evidence; the whole subject was 'exceedingly complex'; estimates by the MRC were 'open to authoritative criticism'; there was indeed statistical evidence to contradict the view that smoking caused lung cancer; and the manufacturers were unaware of 'any carcinogenic substance in tobacco smoke in quantities which conceivably could cause cancer in human beings from smoking'. Their conclusion was:

In the opinion of the manufacturers, there is no proof from any scientific field that smoking is a cause of lung cancer. The statistical evidence certainly does not prove a causal connection. The pressing need is for a comprehensive attempt to close the gap between fact and speculation by further research

- to which the manufacturers would continue to give all the help they could.[45]

In the event the Ministerial statement was made not by Dennis Vosper, the Minister, who was in hospital for an emergency abdominal operation, but by his Parliamentary Secretary, J K Vaughan-Morgan.[46] He easily turned aside pressure from MPs to commit expenditure to the publicity campaign by local health authorities, to ban smoking in public places or take other steps.

The press gave the statement heavy coverage with near-universal emphasis on the fact that (as it was put) people were being left to decide for themselves. (None pointed out that there was never any question of compulsion: the alternative to the Government's passive line was a more vigorous presentation of the facts.) The *Daily Mirror* got out its biggest type for its page one headline: 'SMOKING AND CANCER AND YOU - It's every man for himself!' and had a centre-page spread inside. The *Daily Telegraph* had a two column report on page one and a leader that said the MRC report 'carries the question no further. The evidence remains wholly statistical, and such as it would need no medical knowledge to collect'. It then backed the Government's policy: 'Civilised people are not morons. They know that there are risks attached to most pleasures and duties. Let them know what the risks are, and give them the right to decide whether or not to run them.' The *Daily Express* said 'There should be no question of the Government organising an anti-smoking crusade. The public must be left to make its own choice.' The *Times* was less emphatic but broadly supportive of the Government line, mentioning in particular the need for 'stronger pressure' on the young and raising the possibility of bans on smoking in theatres and other public places.

The exception was the *News Chronicle*, which splashed the story across the whole front page: 'Smokers: It's Up To You - "Cigarettes can kill" Warning' and proceeded to mock Vaughan-Morgan for his unwillingness or inability to answer questions at the press conference about stricter enforcement of the ban on sales of tobacco to under-16s, the idea of smoking bans in public transport and cinemas and theatres, restrictions on tobacco advertising on television, on hoardings or in the press, or advice to GPs on how to deal with patients wanting advice on stopping smoking:

> Here is an example of the tactics of the tall, bespectacled Parliamentary Secretary:
>
> *Do you think lowering the death-rate from lung cancer would be a good thing?*
>
> Well (after a pause) I don't think it would be a bad thing.
>
> *To achieve this will you tell the public they ought to stop smoking?*
>
> I think it is up to the public to make up its own mind from the facts they are given.

In its leading article the *News Chronicle* said: 'This is literally a life-and-death matter, yet the statement in the House was muted to the point of being casual.' The findings needed to be 'hammered home . . . The lead should come from the Government. The subject must be tackled urgently, forcefully, convincingly and continuously.'

The Government was unpersuaded. A circular was issued to local health authorities the day the statement was made[47] and the Ministry of Health again settled down to a period of dogged resistance to the activists who sought more than a circular by way of Government action to warn the public of the dangers of smoking. The baton now passed from the Standing Advisory Committees (and notably Dr Horace Joules) to the local authorities and the CCHE.

Notes

1.   PRO file MH 55.1012

2.   A deputation from the National Society of Non-Smokers (now reborn as Quit), led by their secretary, the Rev. H V Little, went to the Home Office on 6 March 1957 to press for bans on smoking in public places and to protest at the failure to enforce the prohibition on selling tobacco to under-16s - PRO file MH 55.2224. A few weeks later the Home Office replied complacently to a Parliamentary Question on under-age sales that they 'had no reason to think that the provisions [of the law] were not adequately observed' - PRO file MH 55.2220.

3.   PRO files MH 55.1011, MH 55.2232. The MRC also continued friendly contacts with the industry: a note of 29 May 1957 to the Privy Council office records that 'some two months ago we did have a conference with their scientific representatives on the question of research. We shall probably hold others from time to time.' - PRO file MH 55.2220.

4.   BMJ 1954; **i**: 1451-5.

5.   In fact there was little press coverage. (*The Times* (25 June 1954) gave the news six column inches on page 3 under the headlines 'Lung Cancer Inquiry - Doctors' Smoking Habits Analysed'. It spoke of 'further evidence on a likely association between excessive smoking and the occurrence of lung cancer' and mentioned the weaker evidence of an association with coronary heart disease.) This may have been partly the result of work by the tobacco companies: Tony van den Berg, now a member of the Advisory Council of Action on Smoking and Health (ASH) but then personnel director in Godfrey Phillips Ltd and managing director of Markevich Black & White Group, says (personal communication, November 1996) that the companies made full and successful use of their influence as major advertisers to reduce to little or nothing the attention given to the matter in the press. Van den Berg was also chairman of the tobacco industry's National Joint Negotiating Committee and

confirms that the industry used its links with the trade unions to ensure that they too were well briefed with the industry's viewpoint.

6.   Sir Richard Doll gives an overview of the development of the statistical evidence on smoking and the objections raised to it in his article 'Uncovering the effects of smoking: historical perspective' (Statistical Methods in Medical Research 1998; **7**: 87-117).

7.   CHSC(55)6 - May 1955. PRO file MH 55.1011

8.   PRO file MH 55.2220

9.   PRO file MH 55.2232

10.   CHSC meeting on 13 March 1956 - PRO file MH 55.2220

11.   There were Parliamentary Questions on 20 and 26 March and 16 April.

12.   PRO file MH 55.2220

13.   HP(56)49 - PRO file CAB 134.1254

14.   If this policy of inaction pending scientific proof had been pursued to its logical conclusion, it would probably have prevented any action until the publication forty years later of research by M F Denissenko *et al* showing that benzo[*a*]pyrene diol epoxide, found in tobacco smoke, damages the P53 gene in the identical way found in victims of lung cancer: 'Our study thus provides a direct link between a defined cigarette smoke carcinogen and human cancer mutations' - Science 1996; **274**: 430-432.

15.   PRO file CAB 124.1670

16.   HP(56)9th - PRO file CAB 134.1253

17.   CP(56)99 - PRO file reference CAB 129.80 and CM(56)30th - PRO file reference CAB 128.30

18.   The Committee's papers and minutes are all on PRO file CAB 130.115.

19.   Cabinet, 3 May 1956 - PRO file CAB 128.30

20.   PRO file reference MH 55.2232

21.   Sir George Godber, Deputy Chief Medical Officer since 1950, comments (personal communication, 19 January 1998): 'Yes! H[orace] J[oules] used to upbraid me regularly.'

22.   Tobacco Manufacturers' Standing Committee annual reports are available at the PRO for 1956/57, 1957/58, 1958/59 and 1959/60 (PRO file MH 55.2232). They are plainly printed, unpretentious booklets with technical descriptions of chemical research and (in the first report especially) statistical arguments tending to undermine the link between lung cancer and smoking. See also note 44 below.

23. Cabinet paper C(57)135, 4 June 1957 - PRO file CAB 129.87

24. BMJ 1956; **ii**: 1071-1081, 10 November 1956.

25. *Hansard,* 1 March 1957, cols. 1641-1652.

26. *Hansard,* 11 March 1956. The rate was 188 per million in 1945, as stated in the draft MRC statement of 8 March - PRO file MH 55.2232.

27. I have been unable to locate any MRC file relating to the statement, but the draft on the Ministry of Health files is dated 8 March 1956 - PRO file MH 55.2232. It is therefore equally unclear both who in the MRC was responsible for drafting the statement and how the Council approved it - whether at expert, official level or through a meeting of Mr Richard Fort MP and his colleagues. The provenance of the suggestion regarding conclusion (6) of the draft *(see below)* also remains tantalisingly obscure, although one can be forgiven for believing it originated in the Government. The published version of the statement is given in the Appendix.

28. Minute, 28 March 1957, on PRO file MH 55.2220

29. By the end of the month the Ministry's Public Relations and Principal Press Officer, S A Heald, was advising a limited publicity campaign (PRO file MH 55.2203):

> Such an information campaign would save the Government from a charge of having failed to take special steps to ensure that the facts were known and need not cost more than (say) £10-£20,000. This would cover the cost of inserting one or two prominent press advertisements in all newspapers (excluding local weekly newspapers), printing posters and a leaflet.

> This publicity action would be supplemented by Ministerial action - e.g., Parliamentary Statements, answers to Questions, and possibly a Press Conference, and interviews on B.B.C. (sound) and B.B.C. and Commercial Television Services.

> In this way the Government's warning would have been placed prominently on the record, leaving the individual citizen to assess the risk and make his own choice. [There would be follow-up action by] voluntary societies - e.g., Central Council for Health Education - and by youth organisations and education authorities.

30. PRO file MH 55.2232

31. It is unclear from the files I have located who was responsible for these changes - see note 27 above. The revised version of the quoted paragraph reads:

> In scientific work, as in the practical affairs of everyday life,

conclusions have often to be founded on the most reasonable and probable explanation of the observed facts, and, so far, no adequate explanation for the large increase in the incidence of lung cancer has been advanced save that cigarette smoking is indeed the principal factor in the causation of the disease. The epidemiological evidence is now extensive and very detailed and follows a classical pattern upon which many advances have in the past been made in preventive medicine. It is clearly impossible to add to the evidence by means of an experiment in man.

- PRO file MH 55:2232.

32.   The committee, known as GEN 588, had been appointed on 24 April 1956 but had not yet met.

33.   Paper GEN 588/2 - 23 April 1957 - PRO file CAB 130.127.

34.   The same minute by his private secretary recorded that 'the minimum action' to discourage smoking that could be countenanced - but implicitly also the maximum envisaged - was to ask local health and education authorities to 'take whatever action they considered appropriate to make the information known' - PRO file MH 55.2232.

35.   Those present, apart from Butler, were Lord Home (Secretary of State for Commonwealth Relations and Lord President of the Council); Peter Thorneycroft (Chancellor of the Exchequer); Dr Charles Hill (Chancellor of the Duchy of Lancaster); Dennis Vosper (Minister of Health) and Lord Strathclyde (Minister of State, Scottish Office) - PRO file CAB 130.127.

36.   Paper GEN 588/3 - 2 May 1957 - PRO file CAB 130.127.

37.   Dr Hill also quoted Bradford Hill and Doll to cast doubt on the MRC's suggestion that up to 30% of lung cancer deaths might be attributed to atmospheric pollution. The Committee agreed to ask the MRC to re-examine its conclusion. The MRC subsequently amended the reference to say: 'on balance it seems likely that atmospheric pollution plays some part in causing the disease, but a relatively minor one in comparison with cigarette smoking ... A proportion of cases, the exact extent of which cannot yet be defined, may be due to atmospheric pollution.' - GEN 588/4 - 31 May 1957 - on PRO file CAB 130.127.

38.   The CMO took advantage of a WHO meeting to find out what other nations were doing. The USA, Canada, New Zealand, West Germany, the Netherlands, Norway, Denmark, Sweden and Finland were reportedly all concerned and in the main accepted the association of lung cancer with cigarette smoking, though there were doubters who pointed to the possible contribution of atmospheric pollution. 'Statements such as our Ministers have made have been exceptional ... Direct action against smoking under governmental auspices is also very rare': Switzerland had produced a leaflet

for schoolchildren and gave lectures to national service recruits; Sweden had produced a 'small poster on the line of "cut it down".' There was a general tendency to use the voluntary health educational bodies and an inclination to use schools. In Finland smoking was not allowed at 'conferences or committees of a public character' - Appendix B to GEN 588/4, 31 May 1957 - PRO file CAB 130.127.

39. Minute by Sir John Hawton, Permanent Secretary, 8 May 1957 - PRO file MH 55.2232.

40. Letter of 21 May 1957 - PRO file MH 55.2232.

41. Paper GEN 588/4, 31 May 1957, by the Lord President and the Minister of Health - PRO file CAB 130.127.

42. The paper noted that 'the Chancellor of the Exchequer has a number of reservations'. These had been set out at length in a letter the previous day (30 May 1957) from James Collins at the Treasury to P Benner, the Minister of Health's private secretary: 'Our general comment on the statement (which lies behind most of the amendments which we shall be suggesting) is that it goes further than is necessary or desirable; in our view it goes too far beyond the factual description of the situation created by the M.R.C. report; it strays, if I may put it in this informal way, too far into the "missionary field".' The letter attached a list of proposed amendments designed to make the statement as anodyne as possible. - PRO file MH 55.2220.

43. Paper C(57)135 - 4 June 1957 - by the Home Secretary and Lord Privy Seal (R A Butler) - PRO file CAB 129.81.

44. Sir Alexander Maxwell, as chairman of the Tobacco Manufacturers Standing Committee, wrote to Sir John Hawton on 7 June 1957 with the typescript of their first annual report, and about the same time Partridge asked Sir Herbert Brittain at the Treasury for advice about the timing of publication of the report. Brittain consulted Sir John Hawton (11 June), suggesting it should come out before the impending Government statement, and this appears to have been agreed and acted on: six copies of the printed version of the report were sent to Hawton on 19 June. The report ran to 18 pages, emphasising the funding of MRC research and then reporting on the industry's own research. 'The scientists advising and working on behalf of the manufacturers have kept in touch and exchanged information with those working on behalf of the Medical Research Council', it said. Two pages dealt with 3:4-benzpyrene, of which 'only extremely small amounts . . . infinitesimal quantities' were found in cigarette smoke, where it was 'most improbable' that it could be 'in any way injurious'. The report also included a six-page paper by Geoffrey Todd, apparently based on an earlier report by Sir Ronald Fisher, casting doubt on the interpretation of the statistics of smoking and health - PRO file MH 55.2232.

45. Statement to the press, 27 June 1957, included in 'Smoking and Lung Cancer',

3 July 1957 - PRO file MH 55/960.

46.   This was no doubt a matter of relief to Heald, since Vaughan-Morgan, unlike Vosper, was a non-smoker. Heald had minuted the Deputy Secretary on 14 June 1957, presumably with the reports of Iain Macleod's chain-smoking at the 1954 press conference in mind: 'One point is in my view of major importance and involves the Minister's decision. A lot of importance will be attached by the Press and by photographers to whether or not the Minister is seen to smoke or not at the time when this statement is made and immediately thereafter. If he doesn't smoke, though he is known to be a smoker, this will be regarded as highly significant. If he does, on the other hand, it will be regarded as a gesture intended to modify the seriousness of the statement he has made.' - PRO file MH 55.2220.

47.   Copies of circular 7/57 were at the end of July issued also to the Colonies - PRO files MH 55.2224, MH 55.2226.

3

1957-1961:
Masterly Inactivity

For another five years the Government adhered resolutely to their decision to leave any 'propaganda' to the initiative - and expense - of the local authorities, adroitly deflecting all attempts to persuade them into any form of intervention.

The first such attempt came on 12 July, only a few days after the statement in the House. Quoting the Parliamentary Secretary, J K Vaughan-Morgan, who had said in answer to a question after his statement that 'there is no promising line of research which is being neglected for lack of funds', Dr John Burton, the Medical Director of the local authority-financed Central Council for Health Education, wrote to Sir John Charles, the Chief Medical Officer, proposing that research was essential into

> the educational aspects of prevention or early treatment of cancer. . .
> I feel particularly uneasy because of what I consider the unprofessional
> way in which we are approaching the educational side. While many
> hundreds of thousands of pounds are being spent on laboratory
> research it is being assumed that the educational aspects - on which,
> as far as I can see, the whole preventive policy now rests - are to
> operate with no accurate data and as yet no indication of any capital
> investment.

This eminently reasonable proposal set the pattern for the next few years, with the Government prevaricating while local authorities and the CCHE did what little they could to publicise the dangers of smoking.

The CMO referred Dr Burton's letter to the MRC, and Sir Harold Himsworth replied at the end of August. 'I think', he wrote, ' there is some substance in his suggestion that such questions as the reason why people smoke and find the habit difficult to abandon, and the best way to conduct education on the subject, might be investigated.' However, no specific proposals for such work had been put to the MRC, and the area was 'fraught with difficulties for the investigator', being 'uncharted territory between medicine, sociology and psychology, and few techniques have been devised for their investigation'. Himsworth suggested that Burton should be encouraged to pursue his ideas. Sir John Charles scribbled a note on Himsworth's letter: 'Mr Emery - I have spoken to Sir Harold Himsworth about this. In effect it means that the M.R.C. do not consider that it comes within their field. Sir Harold also wonders a little in whose field it might lie. It may be that we will have to look at Dr Burton's proposals 'ad hoc'.' Emery, an Assistant secretary, wrote back to Burton in November seeking 'some elaboration of the plans and possible methods' for the research he had proposed, but by that time the argument had switched to the much more immediate point of money.[1]

In September, Emery had rejected Burton's request for financial assistance from the Ministry, suggesting instead that the CCHE obtain payment in advance for orders for publicity materials placed by local authorities. In October, Burton replied seeking a Ministry guarantee of £1,500 against possible losses on the production of materials. Miss Crawter, the Ministry's Senior Publicity Assistant, recorded her opinion that the CCHE would be able to continue without help, but 'unless the Ministry shows continued interest publicly in this campaign from time to time, local authorities (many of whom are naturally apathetic) will not think the Ministry is in earnest about the seriousness of the warning, and will tend to postpone or drop public education.' Emery nevertheless refused the guarantee. Within days the CCHE complained again about lack of financial support from the Ministry: 'so much capital' - about £1,500 - was locked up in their current stocks of posters (in particular, a leaflet about polio) that all new ventures were blocked. Burton wrote again to Emery on Christmas Eve 1957, complaining that the 'Ministry is being rather hard on us. . . It looks as if we will have to restrict all new publications until March'. Miss Crawter recorded in January 1958 that the 'greatest need' was for a filmstrip for use in schools: Dr Burton was thinking of making it himself so as to reduce the cost to about £60. Burton wrote again in February, saying that the CCHE had been forced to realise £1,000 of its £3,000 investments and run down its stock by 25%.[2]

Meantime, the County Councils Association intervened, writing in January to seek 'a vigorous publicity campaign undertaken by the Government on a national basis on lines similar to the campaign for diphtheria immunisation which proved so successful.' S A Heald, the Ministry's public relations officer, commented that the diphtheria campaign, launched in 1942 at a cost of about £20,000, had cost £60-£70,000 a year from 1945 to 1949 since when it had been run on a reduced scale. It had used local and national press advertisements, billboard posters, films etc. A campaign on this scale on smoking was very unlikely to get Treasury approval 'quite apart from the Treasury's inevitable reluctance to spend money for the purpose of reducing revenue.' Referring to the policy that local health and education authorities should be responsible for the campaign, albeit with Ministry of Health backing, he added: 'It is fair to add that of all the major health problems on which l.h.a.s. *(sic)* have been asked to take action, this is the only one which has not had any direct support from the Ministry in the shape of publicity material or facilities.'[3]

In March 1958, Emery's boss, J P Dodds, the Undersecretary in charge of the Home Health Services Division, addressed the problem:

> My own tentative view is that in the absence of fresh scientific information . . . and in view of the known opposition in some quarters, the luke-warmness in others and the general financial situation, we ought not to think in terms of making any sort of publicity splash. On the other hand, it would be politic for the Minister to be known to be pushing at this subject, even though rather gently . . .

He suggested a £3,000 *ad hoc* capital grant to the CCHE followed up by a circular to local health authorities seeking a report on progress. A S Marre, the Undersecretary for Finance, suggested that the circular should be undertaken first, with a possible approach to the Treasury held in reserve in case the local authority replies showed the present arrangements to be inadequate.

This was the proposal put to the Minister, Sir Derek Walker-Smith, by the Permanent Secretary, Sir John Hawton: 'I am not sure whether you will think this a good moment to stir up this controversial subject again. A progress report would of course help to defend you against any criticism of 'not bothering', but the matter is so quiet now that it might be better to wait and see?' The Minister replied:

> I think perhaps the time is ripe for a new Circular asking for a Progress Report, as suggested. The qn. of financial aid for CCHE is, of course, another matter - with which presumably would be linked the qn. of Govt. responsibility for the contents of publicity material.

When, therefore, in April the County Councils Association sought an answer to their January proposal, Emery's reply referred to the intended new circular and a review of action since the circular of June 1957. The CCA sent another reminder before in July 1958 they and the other local authority associations were consulted on the draft circular, which was not finally issued until 14 August.[4]

Meantime, the tobacco manufacturers themselves had produced two new reports, one citing fifty quotations from experts by which they sought 'to illustrate, by means of extensive quotation from original sources, the conflict of opinion' on the subject. Of the eight experts cited (who included some who were consultants to the industry), three accounted for two-thirds of the fifty quotations.[5] At the same time the TMSC also published 'Smoking and Lung Cancer'[6], a five-page 'interim report', in which they raised questions about (for example) the basis of the statistics (was better diagnosis the origin of the increase?), alleged anomalies (such as the non-smokers who did and the smokers who did not contract lung cancer), and alternative theories involving genetic, psychosomatic and environmental factors. The report concluded with renewed reference to the industry's funding of and cooperation with the Medical Research Council[7] and an assurance much more guarded than an earlier one made by Imperial Tobacco in March 1953 (quoted in note 18 to chapter 1):

> . . . chemical research by the manufacturers continues and will be pressed forward; and if it were ever to reveal the presence of a substance in tobacco smoke in quantities considered likely to be injurious to health every effort would at once be made to remove it or to render it harmless.

Against this discouraging background of official procrastination and industry prevarication, the CCHE and some local authority officials took small steps to educate the public.[8] Miss Crawter, the Ministry's Publicity Assistant, remained vigilant. When a dentist from a Buckinghamshire County Council dental clinic wrote to the Ministry seeking information about lung cancer deaths and Ministry of Health publications on the relationship between smoking and lung cancer she minuted: 'It seems outside the usual dental range'. Miss Forrest, Senior Dental Officer in Dental Health Service, replied: 'Thank you for letting me see this. I agree it is a bit unusual from a dental officer. He appears to have come recently to the Bucks. staff and must be very young as he qualified only last year. Some time, when I meet his chief, Mr Kew, I'll try to find out what kind of lad he is.' Whether the lad received the information he sought is not clear.

Buckinghamshire figured also in a report to a conference of Medical Officers of Health in January 1958: the local Deputy MOH had made 'a papier mâché model of a chinless moron with a cigarette end drooping from his lips called 'Smoky'. These were to be placed in the halls at Secondary Modern (or Grammar) schools . . . the aim was to make the 'smoking boy' look ridiculous.'

> Miss Crawter reported in September 1957 on a CCHE committee meeting:
>
> Dr Burton had the following suggestions: . . . The production of a poster showing a cigarette with the smoke curling from it forming the word 'cancer'. (Another poster headed 'Smoking' and showing a

doctor leaning forward over a table with the footline 'My advice is don't' was turned down by the Chairman of the Committee, Dr Pirrie, after considerable discussion in which I said that it would be 'knocking' the cigarette manufacturers and that in any case the CCHE would get nowhere as the tobacco people had so much money.)

By May 1958 the poster with smoke curling into the word 'cancer' had been banned by the Censorship Committee of the Poster Advertising Industry. The CCHE Fieldwork and Materials Committee were told this was 'because the inference *(sic)* . . . was that one cigarette would cause cancer, which they held to be grossly untrue.' The matter was referred to the local authority associations. When they backed the poster, Miss Crawter minuted her chief:

> Our position on this poster is a difficult one . . . I think the reason offered by the BPAA [British Poster Advertising Association] may be a genuine one, and people are so stupid that there may well be some who would draw the inference claimed by the Censorship Committee. On the other hand, there may be unseen pressures at work. In my opinion we should steer clear of involving ourselves in this matter.

Heald replied: 'I entirely agree with your view . . . any approach we made (if we felt able to do so) would, in my view, be unlikely to have any effect and might even prove embarrassing to the Dept. in certain circumstances.' In October, Miss Crawter was back at the CCHE committee:

> I again drew attention to the interest the tobacco people might have in this poster, and that they might feel the poster was inimical to their interests. (I felt this concealed warning was the most I could do); the unanimous feeling round the table appeared to be that it was fear *[i.e., by the poster industry]* of offending the tobacco manufacturers which was creating this situation.

In August 1958, Dr Scott, the Medical Officer of Health for London County Council, wrote to Dr Goodman at the Ministry enclosing a newspaper advertisement for Churchman's Tipped cigarettes which featured soldiers from the Parachute Brigade and complaining about Army cooperation with the tobacco companies. Dr Goodman wrote to Heald: 'I am rather surprised that Dr Scott should take this up with us which is the sort of thing that some of the less responsible medical officers of health might do!' He sought advice on a reply, adding 'Incidentally, he does not mention the one point which I feel is vulnerable, i.e., the supply of duty-free cigarettes to members of the Services.' Heald took the matter up with the Director of Public Relations at the War Office ('Whatever the circumstances, this sort of thing is, of course, extremely embarrassing as the Government has a rather difficult row to hoe in this particular field') eliciting assurances that allowed Dr Goodman to reply to Dr Scott: 'Further permission [to take photographs of servicemen for advertising purposes] had been in fact refused . . . before our representation was made.'

Two further examples illustrate the ambiguity of the Ministry of Health's position on smoking and the defeatism of their attitude to 'propaganda' - what we should now call health education. The first is their response (November 1958) to a proposal by the National Savings department to refer in a booklet for young people on the virtues of thrift to 'the dangers to health involved in smoking': 'We would not say . . .that smoking was a danger to health without some qualification such as 'heavy smoking'.' The second, the following month, is a minute from Heald to the Undersecretary for the Home Health Services Division, J P Dodds, opposing a Government press advertising campaign which, he claimed, would be impracticable because it 'would only produce a whirlwind advertising 'blitz' by the Tobacco Industry and would get us nowhere. We cannot hope to stop adults smoking . . .' and should therefore concentrate on the young. It could be useful to have a survey of the public to establish that people generally know of the risks of smoking: 'Those who continue to smoke in spite of this knowledge choose to do so as a calculated risk as they have every right to do as they prejudice nobody's health but their own.'[9]

The circular to local authorities issued in August 1958 produced replies which were summarised in a note produced in December:

> Many authorities strongly urge the need for a national propaganda campaign. It is widely felt that what is being done cannot combat the volume of advertising by the tobacco interests, and that the only way to make an impression is to mount a campaign more akin to that undertaken in connection with diphtheria and V.D.

Many local health authorities also wanted enforcement of the under-age sales law by the police and 'prohibition of smoking in cinemas, theatres, restaurants, teachers' common rooms, in public transport, on television and in various other places'.

Dodds discussed the replies with Dr George Godber, one of two Deputy Chief Medical Officers, soon to become a notable Chief Medical Officer but not at this time responsible for smoking policy, and with Heald and others. He then sent a minute through the CMO, Sir John Charles, to the Deputy Secretary, Dame Enid Russell-Smith. The action proposed was minimal: other departments should be informed of relevant suggestions from local authorities; the Ministry of Education should be urged to cooperate ('It is likely that they will require some persuasion'); the Royal Society for the Promotion of Health should be urged to run a seminar at its annual congress. Dr Godber's suggestion that a summary of the local authority replies should be published was rejected because of the embarrassment of rejecting so many suggestions; the 'widespread demand for national publicity' should be met only through the CCHE and not by the Government, but the Ministry should be ready to take up with the Treasury and the Cabinet the question of financial assistance to the CCHE. It was also noted that the Government Social Survey could be used to show that a high percentage of the public already knew of the risks of smoking, thereby taking some of the pressure for more propaganda off the Minister - but it was considered doubtful that a survey was justified simply for this purpose.

The Minister, however, had no such doubts: he agreed the recommendations, such as they were, including the survey, but decided first to consult the Cabinet Home Affairs Committee. His paper[10] made little of the demands for national publicity:

> No new factors have emerged which would suggest that there should be any change in the policy the Government has hitherto pursued, that of limiting its action to making the facts about smoking and lung cancer known and leaving the individual to make up his own mind. My colleagues will no doubt agree that we should continue to base any measures we may take on this general approach.

> There is no positive evidence that the publicity so far has led people to stop or cut down their smoking; indeed, the total consumption of tobacco has gone up. It would, therefore, seem desirable to have a firmer foundation on which to estimate the extent of public knowledge of the risks of smoking, by means of which we can gauge the degree of success of the propaganda measures hitherto employed.

Derek Walker-Smith recommended 'a small scale social survey', noting it might take up to twelve months. 'The survey would probably reveal that [the relevant facts] were fully known to the public', he said at the meeting, 'and this would provide an answer to criticism that further action by the Government was required. In the meantime, a partial answer would be an intensification of the activity in this field of the Central Council for Health Education who might, however, ask for renewed Government assistance for the purpose.' He therefore proposed, as the paper puts it, that 'subject to Treasury agreement, we should not exclude the possibility of making a small financial grant to the Council, if a request therefore *(sic)* is made'.

His colleagues were doubtful about the survey: 'If the survey showed that the public were already fully aware of the facts, it could be argued that little purpose had been served: if, on the other hand, the opposite conclusion were obtained, pressure for a national publicity campaign - to which there were a number of strong objections - would be aggravated.' They agreed to the survey on condition that it should be kept secret until they had been able to consider its results, and in the meantime they rejected any question of a grant to the CCHE.[11]

The survey took rather less than the predicted twelve months and a draft paper on the Social Survey's work was circulated to other departments by the turn of the year. It revealed that a pilot survey addressed to 83 adults and 71 young people had found only one person - 'an old lady of 87, a non-smoker' - had not heard of the association of smoking and lung cancer, and that the full survey had therefore been abandoned. Surveys by the Department of Public Health and Social Medicine of Edinburgh University had found a similar level of knowledge of the alleged connections - but 'that a much smaller proportion accepted that the connection had been proved, and that a negligible number of people had given up smoking because of this.'

The Ministry of Health saw no reason for concern in this last circumstance and circulated a draft paper for the Home Affairs Committee, but the Scottish Office, under the influence of its Chief Medical Officer, Kenneth Cowan[12], now embarked on the path which it pursued for several years, albeit with little obvious result, of urging a more active policy on London. 'We are a little unhappy here at the paper's apparent acceptance that we can do no more to counter the increasing incidence of lung cancer,' they wrote in February 1960: '. . . It might be argued that we have not yet really brought home to the public the risk that smoking involves and the scale of the problem.' The Ministry replied with an amended wording, designed to avoid the appearance of complacency, which the Scottish Health Department felt constrained to accept.

The paper was taken at the Home Affairs Committee on 29 April 1960, with R A Butler in the chair. Echoing the words in his paper, Derek Walker-Smith said at the meeting:

> It was clear that the Government's policy of bringing the facts to the notice of the public (using local health authorities as the main channel of information) had been effective, and that no new departure of policy was required at the present time.

The Committee noted that the CCHE had not renewed their request for financial help and accordingly agreed not to make any grant. The Minister made no reference to a recent letter from the County Councils Association pressing for 'vigorous publicity campaign undertaken by the Government on a national basis' - still less to one from Middlesex County Council to the same effect enclosing a report from their Health Education Officer calling for condemnation of 'the practice of manufacturers exploiting the school boy market with paper packs of [four] cigarettes at a price of sixpence, and the practice of selling single cigarettes in shops.'

Derek Walker-Smith got his way at the Home Affairs Committee, but not without attracting the attention of Lord Hailsham, the Lord President of the Council and Minister for Science, who had been unable to attend the meeting. On 5 May he wrote a cautionary letter to the Minister:

> . . . I have been chewing over the issues raised in your [paper] and am wondering whether we can feel quite happy at leaving the question of

publicity where it stands at present. Can we feel quite justified in accepting a state of affairs in which the public, and particularly the young, are bombarded heavily with persuasions of various kinds to take up or continue smoking, while their education in the risks of smoking is still so limited as at present? There has been a great deal of very useful and difficult work done in evaluating the connection between smoking and lung cancer and I cannot help feeling that we have a responsibility for pushing it very clearly before public notice.

I have noted from the minutes of last Friday's meeting that you are proposing to consider from time to time whether any further stimulus is needed to local authorities in the provision of education on this matter, and I do very earnestly trust that you will agree with me that this is a question which needs watching very closely.

I am sending a copy of this letter to Rab [Butler].

Walker-Smith took ten days to send a soft answer:

While we cannot hope to compete with the tobacco manufacturers in the scale of our publicity - and indeed our declared object is effectively to make known the risks and to leave the individual to decide for himself - I entirely agree that there is a duty on us to see that what is put out is as effective as possible and is directed to the right audience, i.e., the young and those who have responsibility for them.

Hailsham disappears from the record for the next two years - but then returned with a vigorous interest.

Meantime, a significant new player entered the debate. The August Royal College of Physicians, founded in 1518, now made its first intervention in a public health debate since 1725, when it had protested to the House of Commons about the rising consumption of cheap gin.[13] In 1604 when James I published his famous *Counterblaste to Tobacco*[14], the Royal College rejected his proposal that smoking was damaging to health. Now, however, they appointed a committee to look at the effects of smoking and atmospheric pollution on health. Sir George Godber recalls that he and Dr Charles Fletcher, who became secretary and prime mover of the committee, had plotted its creation. Fletcher, who was a member of the Standing Medical Advisory Committee,

had approached me about M[inistry of] H[ealth] inaction. I suggested that he and I should separately approach the new PRCP [President of the Royal College of Physicians], Robert Platt, who was an old friend of mine, and suggest the RCP set up a committee on Smoking and Health. He agreed and wanted me to be a member but I could see that being inhibitory and advised against. I think this was 1958. I told [Sir John] Charles what I had done but pointed out that I was a Councillor of the RCP and this was not a Ministry proposal.'[15]

Platt readily agreed the proposal and indeed chaired the committee and in January 1960[16] Fletcher wrote officially as its secretary to Godber to

ask the Ministry of Health ... what they are actually doing now in respect of the cancer of the lung problem. In particular, what steps, if any, they are taking to assist local authorities with 'health education', and if the Ministry have any evidence of any effect of anything that they are doing.

It took until March for Godber to reply to this enquiry, and the eventual reply was bland:

The Minister's policy is to bring effectively to public notice the risks involved in smoking and to do this through local health authorities . . . The first action was to send a circular to local health authorities in June, 1957, enclosing a copy of the statement by the Medical Research Council . . . and asking authorities to take appropriate steps to bring the facts to notice. No publicity material is provided directly by the Department but suitable material is available from the Central Council for Health Education and elsewhere including, for instance, a film in the Government Central Film Library. The material provided by the Council includes bookmarks, posters and leaflets.[17]

Local authority replies to a follow-up circular had shown that they were concentrating on children and young people. 'The Ministry has no precise information about the effects achieved by publicity . . . ' but published reports showed 'widespread knowledge' although there was 'no evidence that as a result people had given up smoking.' This reply did not satisfy Fletcher and he continued to write over the next few months with detailed enquiries.

In the interval until the Royal College of Physicians finally published their report in March 1962 its anticipated publication was increasingly used by the Ministry of Health as an excuse for inaction - without any concomitant signs of preparation for subsequent action. During this time there are two sequences of papers on the files that provide a striking contrast between attitudes in the Ministry and in the Scottish Office.

First, between December 1960 and March 1961 there are transient signs of disquiet on the part of the deputy secretary, Dame Enid Russell-Smith, about the increase in spending on tobacco advertising and the extent to which it was directed towards the young. Board of Trade figures obtained in December 1960 in order to answer a Parliamentary Question showed that press advertising of tobacco had risen by over 50% in the first three quarters of 1960 compared with the corresponding period in 1959. Dame Enid wrote to the Permanent Secretary: 'I find the increase in expenditure on advertising startling and wonder whether we ought not, after the Questions have been answered, to try to establish how far, as alleged, it is directed at young people.'

She commissioned an enquiry, and in January 1961 a principal in the Home Health Services Division, W M Judd, opined:

> There can be little doubt . . . that the cigarette manufacturers are increasingly directing their advertising at the young. This is obviously so with television advertisements . . . which, with few exceptions, portray physically attractive young couples indulging in the delights of smoking brand X.

He quoted from an editorial in the trade journal *Tobacco* (September 1960):

> The increasing importance of welfare state women, teenagers in particular, as buyers of all manner of produce has become especially marked in recent years in the tobacco trade. As buyers of cigarettes their importance has become more and more emphasised, as anyone who has studied the trend of manufacturers' advertising may be well aware.

and from 'a *Guardian* article . . . which *Tobacco* has reproduced without comment':

> . . . [tobacco] manufacturers seeking to introduce a new brand tend to concentrate their promotional efforts on teenagers and other young smokers, who are not yet set in their ways.

and took the matter up with the Board of Trade, telling them that Dame Enid 'finds the increase in expenditure on tobacco advertising startling'.

Not so the Board of Trade, where another principal, C B Selby-Boothroyd, author in the next few years of many highly opinionated memoranda based on his own sceptical brand of commonsense, replied briefly that no further information was available but that television advertising was 'clearly pointed indiscriminately at the public with no age-bias'.

Judd's boss, the assistant secretary Mrs D M O'Brien, found this a 'rather surprising generalisation' and doubted whether 'the Board of Trade are being as helpful as they might'. She approached them through the Ministry's press office to be told that, following the 'withdrawal of controls on the import and usage of tobacco', they no longer had the close connections with the industry of previous years and were unable to help, although her new informant 'personally would not be so definite' as Selby-Boothroyd about the lack of bias towards young people.

At that stage, however, the Ministry of Health press office was advised by advertising industry sources that 'the inclusion of young people in the advertisement visuals does not restrict the appeal of the advertising to the young' and that under half of those aged 16-24 were 'regularly exposed to commercial television'. 'In summary,' wrote the press office informant, 'I should say that such evidence as we have confirms the Board of Trade view that advertising is pointed indiscriminately without age bias. Its aim is to establish brand loyalties - smoking is so firmly accepted as an adult practice that the tobacco manufacturers see no need to suggest to the young that it be followed but try only to influence the selection of the brand, and this is equally important at all ages.' This argument, promoted by tobacco and advertising industry sources to this day, was taken as the last word: on 1 March, Mrs O'Brien minuted: 'This matter can now rest . . . I am satisfied that the view that the advertising of the cigarette manufacturers is directed specifically at young people is a matter of conjecture and not of known facts . . . '[18]

The narrow focus and perfunctory analysis of this, the most intervention-inclined episode on the Ministry's files for many years, contrasts sharply with a perceptive and well-researched eight-page critique of Government policy with proposals for action that the Scottish Office Health Department submitted to its Ministers (and copied to the Ministry of Health in London) just three months later.

The memorandum's author, T D (later Sir Douglas) Haddow, secretary of the Scottish Department of Health (and later Permanent Secretary at the Scottish Office), started by quoting evidence from polls and prevalence surveys, summarised thus:

> In short, Government policy has apparently succeeded to the extent that it aims to let people know about the possibility of a link between smoking and lung cancer. It has partially succeeded to the extent that it seeks to persuade them to believe that smoking may cause lung cancer. It has failed to the extent that it might have been hoped that the spread of knowledge would reduce the percentage of people who smoked or who started to smoke.

He expressed sympathy with local authorities' doubts about their ability to compete with the 'high-pressure publicity efforts of the tobacco manufacturers' in the absence of strong Government support.

He then quoted WHO figures showing Scotland in first place in a league table for incidence of lung cancer (and England and Wales in second place), referred to the increase in deaths from lung cancer in Scotland, now accounting among men for '1 in 15 of all deaths compared with 1 in 34 in 1950', and the lack of any prospect for a cure for a disease which in 80% of cases was fatal within a year of diagnosis.

He produced a series of sharp criticisms of 'the present policy of encouraging local authorities to put the facts before the individual and leaving him to decide what to do', including that 'people are not usually adult and responsible when they start smoking'; that 'to some extent smoking is a drug addiction' which people could not quit; the overwhelming disproportion of tobacco advertising compared with publicity against smoking, and the evident lack of wholeheartedness of the official campaign.

Saying that 'the evidence against cigarette smoking is certainly no less conclusive than that on which public health action has often been based in the past', Haddow then considered whether a major publicity campaign should be directed only at the young or at the whole population, rejecting the former because lung cancer would be a very remote threat to the young, who might act in defiance of the campaign to 'demonstrate resistance to adult authority', while even if successful it would take 20-30 years to affect the lung cancer rate. Besides, there was evidence that people who quit smoking at any age reduced their risk of developing the disease.

He proposed a £1 million campaign directed at the general public - 'on the scale of 'drinka pinta milka day' ' - which, rather than being expected to reduce consumption greatly by itself, would have as its prime purpose to 'create a climate of opinion in which other action, notably fiscal action, might be possible', for 'it is doubtful . . . if any very large cut in consumption would be made unless the price of tobacco was also raised considerably.' In 1947 a tax-induced price increase from 2s.4d. to 3s.4d. per packet had cut consumption by 15%, but now the price was substantially *lower* in real terms than after that increase in 1947. A 50% increase in tax that resulted in a 30% cut in consumption would still produce an extra £42m. annually, compared with which the cost of the publicity campaign would be small.

The support of the medical profession would be vital and he proposed that its members and Government Ministers should be advised themselves to stop smoking to show the seriousness of their intent. He recognised the political difficulties of his proposals and that there might be some loss of employment in the tobacco industry, but asserted the primacy of tackling 'one of the most important health problems now before us'.

Such clarity of thought (parts of the memorandum could well have been written today) undoubtedly came as a shock to Ministry of Health officials and Medical Officers, who immediately set about neutralising it.[19] Mrs O'Brien proposed that the Scottish Office be warned that 'we would not dismiss as lightly' as they the efforts of local health authorities, 'a trickle' of annual reports from whose Medical Officers of Health was arriving, which would enable them to review whether more should be done. 'We have continued to turn over in our minds what more might be done' but the Scottish ideas were 'a very big advance from the present policy'. Dismissing controls on advertising (which the Scottish Office had not proposed), she called their tax proposals

> quite unrealistic politically and economically. It is one thing to use an increase in tobacco tax for revenue raising or as a regulator, for economic reasons, of the productivity of the industry. It is quite a different matter to seek to disturb the economic structure of an industry to regulate a social habit, however unhealthy it may be.

She asserted that the 'mammoth publicity campaign' would fail to soften up public opinion while the fiscal measures would 'mobilise the opposition of a powerful industry... Moreover, the [Scottish Office] paper makes no reference to ....the effect on national production of depriving workers of tobacco'.

Instead, she tentatively suggested two alternative approaches: advice by the Ministry on how to quit smoking ('I realise that this is liable to raise loud horse laughs from the public but if we were to back it up by the promotion of research for a drug to facilitate the breaking of the habit this approach might carry more conviction') or 'a public pronouncement by the Minister openly condemning the consumption of cigarettes as the cause of disabling and ultimately fatal respiratory diseases and lung cancer... This goes a great deal further than anything that has yet been said but can be fully supported by medical evidence'. Against this she added in manuscript: 'But I suppose that it follows from this that all officials of the Ministry would have to set a good example!'

Her boss, the undersecretary J P Dodds, invited the views of the Ministry's medical and public relations branches. R Goulding, a Senior Medical Officer, commented on the Scottish policy proposals to Dr Goodman, who had been appointed Deputy Chief Medical Officer in 1960: the Scottish approach 'is certainly a bold one but of doubtful practibility *(sic)* ... Before any bold step is taken the backing of the medical profession must be secured and there are still numbers, perhaps a majority of doctors who are not sufficiently convinced that the evidence against tobacco is strong enough for preventive action to be taken, though I feel that a positive statement from the Minister (not the M.R.C.) might help many to resolve their doubts ... I am convinced that a considerable increase in price would do more than anything else to cut down consumption but that the pressure to do this should come from unattached scientific bodies and from the weight of the medical profession (has the B.M.A. any policy on this question?) and not from any official sources.' Before producing his own comments, Goodman asked Goulding: 'Is there - or is there likely to be - any drug which has a significant effect in helping people to stop cigarette smoking? (Short, of course, of a big dose of potassium cyanide.)', getting the prompt reply: 'As yet, and in the foreseeable future, not a hope.' Goodman then produced his comments:

> We have been holding our hand (a) to make sure that diminution in smoking would not come about through the present Government policy ... [I]t is clear that this has not happened. (b) To await some new report, or pressure from outside, which might give a peg on which to hang an initiative.

No new research since 1957 had served this purpose[20], but the report from the Royal College of Physicians committee was expected in October, and there might be merit in awaiting its publication, particularly if we can get the R.C.P. [as against its committee] to make a pronouncement . . . We had also been hoping - quite vainly - that a change in social habits or an increase of taxation on tobacco for other reasons might have had an effect; or that a natural decline in the disease might occur.

Such whistling down the wind having failed, Goodman proposed several concomitant lines of approach: a publicity campaign such as the Scottish Office proposed; 'a large increase in tax'; 'increased pressure to prohibit smoking' in places where it was not allowed in other countries - a matter for local authorities and private concerns; 'provision of, and research on, ways to help people give up smoking' (although a 'deterrent drug' was unlikely); and publicising Doll and Hill's finding 'that the lung cancer rate is reduced if heavy cigarette smoking is given up even after long periods'. In addition, he suggested:

> Since cigarette smoking is known to be more harmful than pipe or cigar smoking, a switch might be effected - with the aid of the pipe manufacturers? i.e., don't be cissy and smoke cigarettes; top people smoke a pipe. (Does the Queen smoke?).[21]

Such a mixture of stray good sense and nonsense from one of the Ministry's key scientific staff contrasts sadly with the professional analysis from Scotland.

From the Public Relations division, Heald produced one of a long line of mildly sceptical but reasonably professional memoranda on ways to run an effective campaign. He was doubtful about tax increases: 'although there is an initial fall in consumption . . . the tobacco addicts soon find the money again. Most of [the young] seem to have money to burn.' As to advertising, 'it would be difficult in principle to justify a selective ban on tobacco advertising without treating alcohol in the same way, although pressure might be exerted to control the form of advertising.'

Summarising, he wrote: 'Example has more influence than publicity', while no publicity campaign 'will have any effect unless the facts can be clearly, simply and forcefully stated without qualifications (which simply provide loopholes for argument and doubt).' However, with such clear advice 'to the young, not to start; to smokers, it is not too late to give up or at least (as a first step) to reduce smoking to not more than a packet a day; to parents, doctors, teachers and organisations, to set a good example in public and especially with the young, then not only will some effect be produced, but the Ministry can feel that it has done all that is reasonably possible and effective in tackling a most difficult problem in regard to which the decision must rest with the individual; in the light of his knowledge and appreciation of the facts and the risks involved (just as he decides whether to fly, or to cross the road in the face of traffic.'

With this internal exchange of views, the Scottish proposals were put on the shelf pending the report from the Royal College of Physicians. Early in September, Mrs O'Brien seems to have discussed possible actions with J P Dodds, but he minuted her 'We agreed that there is nothing useful to be done before the R.C.P. report becomes available', and there is then a series of minutes enquiring when the report is to be published.

There was a new approach at this time from the Tobacco Manufacturers' Standing Committee. Geoffrey Todd, now its Director, arranged to see Sir Bruce Fraser, the new Permanent Secretary, 'in order to explain ... what the manufacturers are doing in the way of research. He does not wish to broach any new grounds or argue a case.' A briefing from an unidentified medical officer says:

> Research activities of the T.M.S.C. appear to have been instituted rather as a defensive programme . . . [An aide-memoire by Todd] rather emphasise[s] the, not unnaturally, biased approach to the subject which is apt to make one slightly hesitant to accept this research project as purely disinterested.[22]

Todd followed up his (unminuted) meeting on 4 August 1961 with a letter to Sir Bruce proposing that the TMSC entertain him and his Minister, now Enoch Powell, to lunch. This led to a flurry of minutes on the file which established that there was no precedent for such a meeting, despite a suggestion by Todd to the contrary. Officials surmised that the request was probably stimulated by expectation of the Royal College of Physicians report, and the Minister was advised to decline the invitation. He did so in a letter of 30 August, alleging an over-full diary.

Six weeks later, Todd was chasing for a reply to a proposal that blood donors be asked whether they smoked, so as to enable an investigation of a possible genetic connection between smoking and a blood group antigen, suggested some years previously by Sir Ronald Fisher, the TMSC's scientific adviser. Dr Goodman noted: 'I know Fisher and his work and I know Todd personally. The latter is relatively harmless but the former is an enfant terrible who is dangerous because of his statistical eminence.' The suggestion was therefore refused.

Todd, however, was still pursuing his personal meeting with the Minister. A letter of 26 October from Martin Madden MP to Powell forewarns him:

> Dear Enoch,
>
> I thought you might like to know that we have invited Mr and Mrs Geoffrey Todd to join us at dinner on Thursday 2 November. Geoffrey Todd is the Director of the Tobacco Manufacturers' Standing Committee which deals with smoking and cancer. The

Todds are old friends and your common interest did not occur to me at the time.

I am certain that Geoffrey Todd will not introduce his 'shop' unless you want to encourage him . . .[23]

It is unlikely, however, that Todd would have gained much from an encounter with Powell, whose powers of analysis would easily have seen through industry prevarications. Indeed, Powell's impatience with slack thinking was soon exercised - but on woolly thinking in the RCP report, not on some industry special pleading.

Notes

1.   PRO file MH 55.2224

2.   PRO file MH 55.2224

3.   PRO file MH 55.2203

4.   PRO file MH 55.2224

5.   *Smoking and Lung Cancer - The Conflict of Opinion,* Tobacco Manufacturers' Standing Committee, London, December 1957. The most quoted expert, with 17 citations, was Dr Ian Macdonald, of the University of Southern California School of Medicine. Dr Milton Rosenblatt, of New York Medical College, was cited nine times, and Dr Harry Greene of Yale University School of Medicine, eight times - PRO file MH 55.2232.

6.   *Smoking and Lung Cancer - Interim Report,* Tobacco Manufacturers' Standing Committee, London, December 1957 - PRO file MH 55.960.

7.   The *Daily Telegraph* reported on 20 January 1959 that grants from the Tobacco Industry Research Committee had reached a total of £1,142,850 - PRO file MH 55.960.

8.   This and the following items are found on PRO file MH 55.960.

9.   PRO file MH 55.2203

10.   H.A.(59)18, 11 March 1959 - PRO file CAB 134.1977.

11.   H.A.(59)Th, 20 March 1959 - PRO file CAB 134.1976.

12.   Previously Medical Officer of Health in Essex - see chapter 1, note 8.

13.   Mentioned in *Dirty Business,* by Peter Pringle, Aurum Press, London, 1998 - an excellent overview of the tobacco industry conspiracy, especially in the USA, that started in the 1950s and has only recently come unravelled.

14.   *A Counterblaste to Tobacco*, London 1604, reprinted in facsimile 1969 by Theatrum Orbis Terrarum Ltd, Amsterdam, and Da Capo Press, New York.

15.   Personal communication, 19 January 1998.

16.   The letter is dated 18 January 1959 but the context makes it plain this was in error for 1960 - PRO file MH 55.2226.

17.   An undated note on the file (probably March 1960) shows the following sales of CCHE materials on smoking for the entire period 1956-59 (with the rider that only in 1958 were all items available throughout the year): two different pamphlets: 196,000 and 43,000; bookmarks: 364,000; five different posters: 19,000, 3,000, 12,000, 2,000, 10,000. - PRO file MH 55.2226.

18.   PRO file MH 55.2227

19.   One way they did so was apparently to keep the Scottish memorandum from George Godber, now Chief Medical Officer: his first knowledge of it was when he read the draft of the present work. (Personal communication, 19 January 1998).

20.   At about this time, the Medical Research Council files reveal their Committee on the Aetiology of Lung Cancer being consulted by Austin Bradford Hill and Richard Doll 'on whether they should extend their prospective survey of about 40,000 members of the British medical profession, begun in 1951, beyond the 10-year limit now approaching. For the survey to maintain its value in relation to the aetiology of lung cancer it would be necessary to make arrangements for requestioning the participants about every five years and this was a heavy task. The Committee were unable to offer any positive advice since while they thought the prolongation of the survey might yield interesting information, they could not be sure that the labour involved would be proportionate to the value of the results.' - PRO file FD 1.7792.   In the event, of course, the research continued, and Richard Doll, with his new collaborator Richard Peto, was gloriously able to publish in 1994 his forty-year follow-up report, showing that regular smoking kills about half those who indulge in the habit and does so through at least 24 diseases - BMJ 1994; **309**: 901-11.

21.   PRO file MH 55.2227

22.   PRO file MH 55.2232. The same short note states how valuable the TMSC's statistical papers were proving - the industry, however, discontinued publication of them after 1985, when economic analysis of tax increases was becoming more prominent in tobacco control and Treasury thinking.

23.   PRO file MH 55:2232

4

1961-62:
The Report of the
Royal College of Physicians

At the end of July 1961, the Ministry of Health undersecretary J P Dodds asked Dr Neville Goodman, the Deputy Chief Medical Officer, whether a preview of the Royal College of Physicians report might be possible. Dr Goodman responded:

> Alas! the report and its contents are 'secreta Collegia'. CMO has seen and let me - as another Fellow - have a quick glance but if we were to let the Dept. have it we are probably liable to some frightful penalty (?drawing and quartering) under an Act of Henry VIII! I can only say that I think it will give us the needed springboard.

Nevertheless, a draft was circulated in the Ministry on 1 November: Sir George Godber recalls: 'Charles [Fletcher] sent me the draft report and I got Enoch Powell to read it and be ready'.[1] The draft was officially submitted to the Minister by Sir Bruce Fraser with a covering minute:

> So clear and comprehensive a report from so authoritative a source is bound to make a considerable public impression and the Government will of course be pressed to say what attitude they take to the report in general and to the suggestions for Government action in particular. Of these suggestions the first (more health education) and the last (anti-smoking clinics) are the business of the Health Departments

and he referred to the suggestions the Department of Health for Scotland 'have been working up' before continuing:

> It seems to me that the Government collectively must at least reconsider the question . . . Hitherto the general policy has been [to publish the facts but] that the choice of action should be left to individuals, since the Government ought not to be too grandmotherly. The dividing line depends, of course, on the degree of the health hazard. Drugs of addiction are banned, tobacco and alcohol are not . . . I think it is difficult to resist the argument that the Government ought to take more strenuous publicity action, particularly in respect of children. Beyond that it can be said that if people choose to smoke themselves to death (or drink themselves to death or work themselves to death) freedom of choice should prevail.

He suggested that 'it would be as well at an early date, in conjunction with the Scots, to bring the conclusions of the report to the attention of the Home Affairs Committee [of the Cabinet] so that the Government may be ready with their reaction when, or shortly after, the report is published.'

Powell scarcely referred to these points but focussed directly on what - as he correctly surmised - is the single most powerful means of reducing tobacco consumption: price. He quoted scathingly from the report:

> 'It seems unlikely that increased taxation would have any lasting deterrent effect' (para. 117). A statement so patently wrong in a Report of such general carefulness and detachment as that of the Royal College of Physicians is breath-taking. How many packets of cigarettes would be sold if the duty was £1000 - or £50 - or £1? . . .

> The Government has it in its power, without prohibition or interference directly with anyone's freedom of choice, to cut cigarette smoking whenever and to whatever extent it pleases. Indeed, given the probable flatness of the demand curve, they could combine a big cut in consumption with no reduction, and possibly an increase, in revenue. If duty were increased for explicitly public health reasons, the odium would be much less than with ordinary increases of taxation, and it would be possible to use a cost-of-living index which excluded tobacco. . .

> In my opinion if the Government is unwilling to use this power - was it not the method used against gin (para.2)? - then health education and all the rest is merely humbug and will be felt and seen to be such. In any case, 'health education' has already gone a long way (paras. 106, 108) without producing the slightest effect, and I don't believe advertising makes any difference one way or the other.

> The publication of the Report will excite temporary interest and for weeks afterwards we shall have to answer a shower of tiresome

> Questions about what the Government is not doing; but unless my colleague [i.e., the Chancellor of the Exchequer] is prepared to use the fiscal weapon, I personally propose to indulge in as little humbug as I can get away with.

He concluded by suggesting a high-level meeting with the Treasury.

Fraser replied with the department's customary but determined moderation. When he had suggested 'more strenuous publicity action' he had not had in mind anything as substantial as the £1m. campaign the Secretary of State for Scotland, in a draft paper just to hand, was now suggesting. He concentrated his fire, however, on his own Minister, who was showing dangerous signs of stepping out of line. It was not possible, he wrote, to maintain that 'a really swingeing increase' in tax did not interfere with anyone's freedom of choice:

> All sorts of objections can be raised against taxing the habit virtually out of existence. Interference with freedom of choice and with established social customs, savage damage to an almost major manufacturing industry and the investors therein, unemployment among the industry's employees and - politically perhaps more significant - damage to the livelihood of many small shopkeepers, increase in the cost of living index and consequent pressure for higher wages, all suggest themselves; and I think the decision will be seen to be more difficult on political than on fiscal grounds. Hence I am sure that it should be brought before Ministers collectively as soon as possible.

> One has to reckon with the possibility that Ministers will not face the odium of a crushing increase in tax. You clearly will not be able to take the attitude, either publicly or with your colleagues, that because the Chancellor has not taken the drastic action which you would have liked and which would, in your view, have rendered other action unnecessary, you are therefore excused from taking such minor action as is open to you in your own field. I think, therefore, it is our duty to be considering what we could usefully do by way of further publicity, anti-smoking clinics, or the like. There will be heavy pressure on you (and on any other Ministers who may have minor contributions to make) to enable these measures to be dressed up as forming together an adequate Government policy in the face of the threat to health. Here no doubt is where the danger of humbug will come in.

Even so soon before the Report was published, concern at the highest official level in the Ministry was with appearances rather than reality.

The year ended with a flurry of calls to control tobacco advertising. Thomas Galbraith, a junior Scottish Office minister, asked for a brief on this (and on the industry's progress in making safer cigarettes) and was discouraged on both fronts. Francis Noel-Baker MP pressed in correspondence with the Board of Trade and the Post Master General (Reginald Bevins) for a ban on television advertising during the hours children were watching, or else altogether as with advertising for spirits and was told the former could not be defined while there was no ban on advertising spirits, only 'a gentlemen's agreement about cut-throat competition'.[2] Italy was reported to be introducing a ban on tobacco advertising.[3] The *BMJ* urged that there was 'a strong case for curtailing tobacco advertising', alleging a precedent in Sweden[4], as well as controls on smoking on public transport and in cinemas and theatres and enforcement of the law banning sales to under-16s. The BMA published 100,000 copies of a booklet *Smoking - The Dangers*, and Dr George Godber, now Chief Medical Officer, featured warnings about smoking in his first annual report.[5]

Anticipation of the Royal College report was driving tobacco share prices down, as cuttings on Board of Trade files reveal, and the industry needed to step up its lobbying. A minute by Sir Frank Lee, the joint permanent secretary at the Treasury, to Sir Thomas Padmore, second secretary, reports that Partridge, now Deputy Chairman and Managing Director of Imperial Tobacco, 'came to see me this afternoon' (21 February 1962) to ask to which Ministers they should send their comments on the forthcoming report. (Personal contact is so much more effective than a telephone enquiry, let alone consulting a yearbook!) The Board of Trade's permanent secretary, Sir Richard Powell, received a copy of the minute and wrote:

> We are of course so heavily dependent upon revenue from tobacco, which is now £880 million a year, that anything that seriously affected this revenue would be a very serious matter for the Chancellor. My own guess is that there will be a severe and immediate impact, the effect of which will gradually wear off, and that there will be a further drive towards filter tips. I doubt however whether there will be any serious permanent loss of revenue, but even if there is the public will soon find something else on which to spend its spare money, and this will no doubt be vulnerable to tax in some way.[6]

However, the Treasury had by mid-January 1962 already convinced itself that the Health Department was sufficiently under control not to rock the tax boat: with a proposal coming forward to abolish the licensing of tobacco retailers, Sir Frank wrote to the Chancellor's private office:

> As you know, I am becoming much more doubtful about whether (a) we shall be getting far reaching proposals from the Minister of Health and the Secretary of State [for Scotland], (b) even if we do, whether they will be accepted by the Government (i.e., in the form of fiscal measures).

I would therefore go ahead with this harmless reform 'regardless'. We could always back-track before the Budget if there were a real campaign against smoking (though the maintenance of the licensing system would not really help such a campaign, except very marginally.'

What was happening in the Ministry of Health? Early in January Enoch Powell received a strong note from his colleague David Eccles, the Minister of Education:

I must declare my interest. I have the medical profession in my blood and my younger brother has died of lung-cancer. He was a heavy smoker.

Eccles had read the advance copy of the RCP report; he thought it obvious that 'the tobacco manufacturers have recently been aiming their advertisements more and more at young people' with messages that not smoking was 'square' and that linked smoking and romance; and

I want to be ready to go into action when the Royal College of Physicians' Report comes out. Could we discuss this?

A day later Powell met John Maclay, the Secretary of State for Scotland, and they

agreed that the next step should be the preparation at official level of a publicity scheme from which it would be possible to judge how much could effectively be done without other Government action. The assumption would be a campaign not merely supported by but largely conducted by Central Government . . . It would be necessary to consider whether such a campaign could be confined to plugging of the facts without spilling over into direct exhortation on the Government's behalf to cut down or give up smoking.

Sir Bruce Fraser ends his note of the meeting by recording that a paper was to be quickly prepared for the Home Affairs Committee of the Cabinet and 'shown to the Treasury in the ordinary way'.

He attached to his note a two-page plan for a publicity campaign that the Scottish Office had handed over at the meeting. It called for discussions with the medical profession to ensure their cooperation (something which never happened throughout the period under review) followed by a two-stage publicity campaign, first briefing 'those who influence opinion' including Ministers, local authorities, trade unionists, employers, teachers, clergy, leaders of voluntary organisations and others, then using TV, press and poster advertising, editorial support in the media, etc., leading on to local authority bans on smoking in public places and advice on how to stop smoking, including 'stop smoking clinics'. It envisaged the need for full-time qualified staff.

By contrast with the strategic thinking of this plan, however outline in form, the mood at an internal Ministry of Health meeting that Sir Bruce called on 15 January 1962 was already defensive and thinking was on a small scale. 'The most obvious feature at present was the sense of defeatism among local authorities. They had not been given a national lead since 1958 and their educational and advertising efforts were puny . . . horrific posters were now more acceptable to the public [but] the only free sites likely to be available were in public conveniences' (to which is added in manuscript 'and perhaps GPs' surgeries'). 'It would cost £50,000 p.a. to have an effective poster campaign against smoking. It would obviously be desirable to have television advertising too, if the I[ndependent] T[elevision] A[uthority] was prepared to grant time to opposition to one of its chief sources of revenue' but this would cost £52,000 p.a. for one minute a week. Sir Bruce put off any thought of television advertising until after the Government had considered prohibiting tobacco advertising on TV. Overall, however, any publicity campaign faced major obstacles: the RCP report (according to the note of the meeting) 'was full of loopholes', the Scottish Office plan was unsound in parts; and (amazingly) 'there was still no proof of the smoking-cancer connection'.

Heald, the Ministry's public relations expert, then wrote a long memorandum. Having stated that he was not a smoker himself, he made a number of preliminary points, including that the RCP report was too technical, qualified and ambivalent to provide the basis for unequivocal statements such as were needed. 'Publicity starts, therefore, with a tremendous deadweight of handicap; any advertising is bound to be countered by an increased volume of advertising by the tobacco interests as long as such advertising is allowed' - and there was little chance of getting parents, doctors and teachers to stop and so set a good example (actually the 'increasing tendency of doctors to be non-smokers' had been noted at Sir Bruce's meeting). He outlined possible campaigns costing £20,000, £123,000 or £800,000 but went on:

> It is difficult to resist the view that the attempt to change a widespread popular habit which involves three-quarters of the male population (and an increasing proportion of the women) and which in many cases amounts to what is virtually an addiction, would in the absence of what would be generally regarded as clear and positive proof that smoking inevitably causes lung cancer and other diseases, be doomed (in my considered opinion) to failure.

It was therefore 'hard to justify the vast sums envisaged' (in an £800,000 campaign) especially as

> the tobacco interests would not be idle during this time and would undoubtedly take up the challenge by doubling their advertising expenditure and public and press relations activities . . . There would undoubtedly be a massive counterattack launched by the tobacco

interests with counterarguments as skilful as they would be insidious, which might succeed in raising fresh doubts and call for retaliation on an equally large scale. The question in my mind is whether the Government can base convincingly and justify the necessary action which will be unpopular upon an interpretation of the facts rather than upon obviously proven facts which speak for themselves and admit no argument (at least in the mind of the man in the street and in the factory).

Dame Enid Russell-Smith forwarded these ideas to the Permanent Secretary, adding her own judgement that a major campaign could not be justified unless 'there were a real chance of effecting a marked change in national smoking habits' - which there was not. Instead, there should be a small-scale campaign directed at parents and student teachers. 'Doctors' waiting-rooms would be splendid sites' for posters - 'moreover the Tobacco Companies could not follow us here!' (The idea of the industry undertaking massive counter-publicity to any Government campaign is found time and again on the files, often advanced as a good reason for doing nothing.)

She then set out the limits on Government action to compel changes of behaviour. 'So far, broadly speaking, the State has not sought to compel anyone to stop doing harm to his own health . . . Although lack of exercise is said to be the cause of much illness in middle life, we have not followed Mussolini in compelling senior Civil Servants to take part in athletics . . .' As with alcohol, 'the regulation relating to drugs of addiction . . . also appear *(sic)* to be aimed at the social consequences just as much as at the safeguarding of health.' It would be a new departure to argue from the cost to the National Health Service of self-damaging behaviour and while such a line of argument might seem reasonable it would not stop at smoking: action on alcohol could be similarly supported and the 'the powerful anti-drink lobby in the Blue Riband movement, The Independent Order of Rechabites, etc., . . . could be counted on to push it.' By contrast there was 'very little in the way of an anti-smoking lobby' - in fact, 'the most effective measure to limit smoking' might well be 'the promotion of a voluntary anti-smoking movement'. (Action on Smoking and Health was not to be founded until 1971, when the Royal College of Physicians produced their second report on the subject, while the National Society of Non-Smokers was less concerned with smoking than with what is now called passive smoking.)

Dame Enid ended by countering Enoch Powell's reference to the 'fiscal and regulatory measures . . . taken in 1751 to limit the consumption of gin', referring to G M Trevelyan to suggest (in a way difficult to read in Trevelyan's own words) that the subsequent fall in gin drinking 'may have been at least in part due to the supplanting in popular favour of gin by tea, which also carried a heavy duty at the time . . . No likely substitute [for smoking] has so far appeared. Even a voluntary movement is unlikely to get very far by pushing chewing gum as an alternative.'

Sir Bruce then sent the papers to Enoch Powell with a sharp reminder of the current Government policy of relying on local authorities and warning him against unilateral action such as he had apparently suggested was within his Departmental competence:

> I do not think, with respect, that this view is sustainable. Any Government campaign, however modest, requires a decision to change existing policy and I do not think you are entitled to go ahead without such a decision consciously and collectively taken.

'Complete consideration of all the possibilities' for Government action was indeed 'likely to be a very prolonged process' but the Health and Education Ministers might be able to get agreement to going ahead alone 'provided that Treasury authority is forthcoming for the spending of money' - although 'it might be objected that to spend even £20,000 would be a waste of money in the absence of those other Government measures, without which, as you made plain in your paper, a publicity campaign, whether modest or elaborate, would have little effect.' A modest campaign directed at schoolchildren was acceptable, but the Treasury, the Board of Trade and the Ministry of Labour would need to be consulted: 'once you get the Government's feet wet . . . it is going to be difficult for the Government to keep the rest of its body dry.' When the Royal College of Physicians report came out, the line might be (subject to his colleagues' approval) that 'on health grounds the Government agree with the proposition that cigarette smoking ought to be discouraged' but the report's 'suggestions for Government action raise wide issues, on which the Government have not yet reached a conclusion' save to go ahead with the campaign for schoolchildren.[8]

Powell, Eccles and Maclay had already two days earlier circulated an anodyne paper to the Cabinet's Home Affairs Committee. It quoted the Royal College report's conclusions and recommendations[9] and attached a paper by officials outlining possible publicity campaigns costing £20,000, £125,000 or £1 mn. The Ministers stated their intentions for a school- and parent-focussed campaign at a cost of about £20,000, but added that 'no publicity campaign, however costly or elaborate, would by itself have more than a strictly limited effect' unless the Government also took 'such other measures as lie to their hand to reduce the present level of consumption of cigarettes.'

> The matter is clearly one of great social, political and indeed industrial importance, and our colleagues will wish to consider it on broad lines. As the Ministers responsible for the health and education services, we feel that we must urge strongly the case for the Government to use all the practical means in their power to discourage smoking, particularly of cigarettes.

When the paper was discussed, the Home Affairs Committee recognised the pressure likely to come on the Government for action but decided that the recommendations in the report 'would present serious difficulties and it would be advisable to avoid any commitment to give effect to them without further closer examination of their implications.' The Cabinet had to be forewarned of the report; meantime, it was decided to set up a committee of officials to consider the whole subject.

The Cabinet paper - by R A Butler, the Home Secretary - proposed answers to Parliamentary Questions that might buy time for further consideration of the broader topics. The Minister of Health would reply that he and the Secretary of State for Scotland would

> shortly be asking the local health authorities to use all channels of health education to make the conclusions of the Report known and to discourage smoking on health grounds, particularly of cigarettes. We shall be giving them guidance and providing them with publicity material. We are also consulting with the Central and Scottish Councils for Health Education about ways in which they can help.

The Minister of Education would make a similar reply about seeking the cooperation of local education authorities and teachers to make the dangers of smoking clear to schoolchildren 'and to discourage the formation of the smoking habit'.[10]

In discussion at Cabinet, the 'new departure' of taking action 'to check habits which, indulged in to excess, would endanger health' was remarked on as a departure from the policy of leaving decisions to 'the judgement of individuals'. Moreover

> The present revenue from tobacco amounted to over £800 million a year. Any action likely to lead to a sudden and substantial reduction in this figure would need to be considered in its fiscal as well as in its political and health aspects.

The draft Parliamentary Answers were approved - but two days later Selwyn Lloyd, the Chancellor of the Exchequer, had had second thoughts:

> He feared that, if the Government publicly committed themselves to a policy of 'discouraging' adults from smoking, this might prejudice the consideration . . . of the further measures contemplated in the Report . . . After discussion it was agreed that it would be preferable that the Government should not at this stage appear to be assuming a responsibility for 'discouraging' adults from smoking

and the draft Answers should be amended accordingly, along with the circulars to local education and health authorities.[11]

The Government had had advance copies of Royal College report for four months and had deferred action for months before that until the report could provide a suitable peg. Yet this was the state of readiness of the Government when the report was finally published on 7 March 1962. And within two days there was even a quarrel between the Ministers of Health and Education, the latter (Heald warned Sir Bruce) seeing the issue of posters by the Ministry of Health as a trespass on his territory and demanding that no posters should be issued before 'careful study . . . even if this meant a delay of weeks or even months'. The quarrel was not resolved until 20 March.[12]

By contrast the tobacco companies were characteristically well prepared. On 2 February their 'chief research scientist' Dr Bentley had been on television announcing the formation of an industry biological research unit: 'If any harmful substance should be discovered in cigarette smoke, they are confident they would be able to remove it by modifying the cigarette or altering the manufacturing process.' The Board of Trade, which was the industry's sponsor ministry and had close connections with it, in briefing its ministers on the report, managed to combine criticism of its 'obscurities' and doubts about the effectiveness of its recommendations, given the robustness of demand which had increased annually for the last eleven years despite cancer scares, with self-contradictory but lurid warnings about the revenue implications, the dangers for Rhodesia, the risk to the jobs of 40,000 tobacco workers and (more serious) 'the effect on the 427,000 licensed retailers many of whom depend on small shops'. The brief noted the absence from the report of the possibility of a safer cigarette on which 'we know . . . (from Mr Partridge of Imperial) that the manufacturers are arranging to spend a good deal of money'.[13]

When the report came out, the industry (to whom the College had with an old-fashioned but misplaced sense of fair play given an advance copy) issued three documents simultaneously. A two-page press release summarised a five-page statement from the Tobacco Advisory Committee. These supported (as the industry always does) the law banning sales to under-16s, played down the amount of tobacco advertising ('only $1\frac{1}{2}$d in the £ of retail sales, compared with 3d in the £ for all consumer goods and services' - a manuscript annotation on the Ministry of Health file notes that if tobacco tax was excluded the spend was equivalent to about 6d in the £), criticised as inequitable any increase in tobacco tax ('it would penalise the many millions of smokers who derive pleasure and solace from smoking and who, as the report shows, do not develop the diseases in question') and mocked the report's muddled recommendation to print on cigarette packets the nicotine and tar contents, quoting the report itself as saying that 'no claim should be made that any particular brand of cigarette was safer than any other'.

The third document was a 52-page printed commentary by Geoffrey Todd as 'Director, Tobacco Manufacturers' Standing Committee for Research into the Effects of Smoking on Health'. This, with a wealth of miscellaneous statistics and quotations, sought to cast doubt on the effects of smoking on health (except in a vulnerable minority whom research should be directed to identifying) and to condemn air pollution as the main culprit. 'Sir Ronald Fisher has claimed that genotypic factors and air pollution by themselves adequately account for the incidence of lung cancer. . . [and] that the evidence against air pollution is more complete than that against smoking'. Research should also concentrate on the biological effects of tobacco smoke 'so that the precise effect, if any, on the heart and respiratory system' could be ascertained.[14]

The Royal College report nevertheless attracted extensive press coverage and intense public interest. At the Imperial Tobacco annual general meeting later in the month the chairman, R W Clarke, was moved to deplore the volume of 'singularly ill-informed . . . public comment' and went on to emphasise the *bona fides* of the industry ('the tobacco manufacturers . . . fully recognise their responsibility to the public') and their devotion to further research ('many questions yet to be answered; . . . general condemnation of cigarette smoking is neither justified nor constructive').[15] (Research was and remains the industry's constant excuse for perpetual procrastination.) The *Financial Times* reported a week after the College's report came out that cigarette sales were down by 5-10% (while sales of pipe tobacco and cigars, given a relatively clean bill of health by the report, were up), and that tobacco shares had fallen; on 3 May it reported that filter cigarette sales had risen 10% in eight weeks, lifting their market share from 17% in June 1961 to 26%. In a leading article the paper called for a Government campaign of 'education and assistance' directed at adults as well as children and for the industry to moderate its advertising. It said that despite the fact that tobacco tax accounted for 14% of total public revenue, 'the financial aspect of the matter must firmly be given second place. The tax on cigarettes must be raised - not by a small amount . . . but by an amount so large as to risk an actual loss of revenue.' Nearly two dozen Parliamentary Questions found their way onto Ministry of Health files between March and July.[16]

In mid-April, Heald, the Ministry's public relations chief, produced an assessment:

> The influence of the R.C.P. Report and of Government statements and action on public opinion has been remarkable and has gone much farther and faster than might have been anticipated. There are probably two reasons for this: (a) the Press have been greatly impressed by the action of the R.C.P., a body which is rarely in the limelight and never seeks it, in setting up an authoritative committee and in that committee's three years work on the subject; in fact they accepted the main conclusions of the Report without seeking to pick holes in it; (b) the statements made by Ministers and Government

spokesmen and the evidence of Government concern seen in the issue of posters and the promise of more to come has brought home to the public that the Government means business this time and that they should treat the matter seriously.

The problem is to maintain the impetus and the snowball effect of the public relations campaign. This will not be easy and will involve a continued effort of stimulation of local authorities, schools, youth clubs, parents/teachers associations, women's organisations and other voluntary bodies . . .

He proceeded to argue for additional staff in the Public Relations division, concluding that

if the impetus of the public relations campaign . . . can be satisfactorily maintained difficult though this may be, and we succeed in getting a movement going in schools, youth clubs and voluntary bodies, where direct access to the audience is possible and where it is not possible for the tobacco interests to mount a direct counter-offensive, then a commercial advertising campaign can be held in reserve either for the purpose of a counter-attack, if and when the tobacco interests retaliate with a massive onslaught, or if all goes well to clinch the argument and consolidate the successes gained.[17]

But that is to anticipate. On 12 March Enoch Powell found himself pressed hard at Question Time (in particular by Frank Allaun, Marcus Lipton and Kenneth Robinson[18]) on lack of resources for smoking prevention, the inadequacy of official publicity (in particular the failure to use television and press advertising), the need to ban cigarette advertisements on television and to act on poster industry censorship of anti-smoking posters.[19] The next day saw similar points raised in a short debate in the House of Lords, which was answered in conciliatory tones by Lord Hailsham.[20] Simultaneously the Chancellor of the Exchequer, Selwyn Lloyd, announced in the House of Commons that the Treasury found significant problems in the Royal College of Physicians' recommendation for differential taxation of cigarettes and of apparently safer forms of smoking such as pipes and cigars since tobacco was taxed as leaf on import into the UK rather than as manufactured products. When the Budget came on 9 April Lloyd, giving as reasons the cost of a change and the risk of smokers avoiding tax by making their own cigarettes at home from pipe tobacco, left the tax unchanged at 3s.4d. on a pack costing 4s.6d.[21]

Back on 12 March BBC television devoted its *Panorama* programme to the report, and the Ministry of Health obtained a transcript. Richard Dimbleby showed a cancerous lung and quoted Enoch Powell stating in Parliament that afternoon that the Government accepted 'that the Report demonstrates authoritatively and crushingly the causal connection' between lung cancer and smoking - no further prevarication about the causal nature of the connection -

and gave figures for the risks of smoking ('a 20-cigarette a day man has 16 times more risk of dying [of lung cancer than a non-smoker], and a 40-cigarette a day man is 29 times more likely to die . . .'). 'Now about six weeks - in fact exactly six weeks ago today,' Dimbleby continued, 'I gave up cigarette smoking myself after smoking about 40 a day,' - too late, of course, we now know, as he died from lung cancer less than four years later. He talked to a doctor who was running a pioneering anti-smoking clinic and to some of his clients and contrasted the millions spent by the industry on advertising with the £5,000 allocated by the Government to warn people of the dangers.

Robert Kee then interviewed E J ('John') Partridge, billed as chairman of the TMSC, and Sir Robert Platt, the president of the Royal College of Physicians and chairman of its committee. Partridge said he did not accept the 'sweeping assertions' in the report or Enoch Powell's assessment of them. When Sir Robert said that 'we must stop young people smoking' Partridge would not agree and called instead for research on the characteristics of those who proved vulnerable to lung cancer, on air pollution and laboratory studies of the effects of tobacco smoke. Platt replied effectively that the research had already been done - on living populations. Lung cancer in his youth was a rare disease, and 'the personal characteristics of the British race' had not suddenly altered in the past 40 years. Partridge said the industry was 'prepared to sit down with you, or anybody else, and try to map out really constructive research into the thing. I don't believe that your approach, if I may say so, is either constructive or realistic', and the interview ended in a clash between him and Platt on tobacco advertising, Partridge defending advertising: 'to young people?' - 'Yes indeed . . . but not to children' - 'to young ladies?' - 'Certainly, when they reach the age of discretion' - and finding himself in difficulty saying why he did not want children to smoke 'if there's nothing harmful about smoking'.

The number of papers on the files now proliferates many times over as the subject of smoking and health was placed firmly on the agenda of many Whitehall departments for months to come. This was the work of the interdepartmental committee of officials created by the Home Affairs Committee before the report was published. Through it departments attempted to pursue largely defensive interests but were driven from above by a Cabinet minister who, contrary to all past precedent, showed real interest in getting results.

This interdepartmental committee had been reinforced by the Cabinet which, at its own pre-publication discussion, it 'took note that the Prime Minister would arrange for the Departments concerned to carry out a detailed study of the further measures recommended in the Report'. Harold Macmillan wrote on 15 March to Lord Hailsham, the Lord President of the Council, asking him to preside over a 'group of Ministers' to oversee this study. He continued: 'I have asked Sir Norman Brook [the Cabinet secretary] to arrange for a more searching enquiry to be made by officials into the administrative and legal aspects of the recommendations' and suggested that the Ministerial group should not meet until their report was forthcoming. 'But you may like to discuss with Sir Norman Brook the precise field which you would wish the report by officials to cover and the way in which you would like the work handled.'

Hailsham reacted with enthusiasm. His copy of Macmillan's memorandum (written from Admiralty House while no 10 Downing Street was being renovated) bears in his elegant italic hand this note to his office:

> Obviously I must do this. I shall want to interview the secretŷ of the orgñ as soon as poss. I sh want copies of the report on both desks and for home. I shall want to draft a series of questions for the Committee. Pse bring me existing Cab Papers to work on th weekend. I take it the fact of this Cee will <u>not</u> be public.

The secretary of the officials' committee was A L M Cary from the Cabinet Office. Hailsham saw him within a few days, and what he said can be surmised from two (similar) manuscript lists on the Lord President's file. The second reads:

The facts
Further scope for research
  How to keep facts before public
  The young. Schools. Local Health Auths.
  Tax
  Sales. Age 16 too young? ?Power to move slot machines enforced?
      Enforcement
  <u>Advertising</u>
  ?Limitation
  ?Persuasion ?Filters ?Cigars ?Pipes
  ?Tax or Levy
  ?Hoardings
  ?TV. ?hours
  ?Newsp.
  <u>Doctors</u>   <u>Life Insurance Cos?</u>
  <u>Clinics</u>   <u>Churches?</u>   <u>Voluntary Societies?</u>[22]

Cary's committee[23] comprised representatives of the Home Office, Scottish Office, Board of Trade, Treasury, Central Office of Information and Ministries of Health and Education. He circulated a paper to them proposing that they produce a factual report, without recommendations (which were the realm of the Ministerial committee) and sketched its scope: education of children and adults; restriction of advertising ('It has already been suggested that a Government publicity campaign would be ineffective (and I would personally add undignified) unless it is linked with some restriction on advertising by the tobacco companies. This is a subject which bristles with difficulties'); restrictions on smoking in public places and on sales to the young; taxation (including the effect of 'a sudden and sharp reduction in our imports of tobacco from the Colonies, the Commonwealth, or the United States'); smoke analysis, filtration and labelling of packets; and anti-smoking clinics.

Hailsham reacted immediately, and the committee's second paper relayed his comments on Cary's agenda. The Committee should consider under public education not only what schools and local health authorities could do but also the role of 'churches, youth clubs and services, social workers, doctors and insurance companies'. Questions on advertising should include whether restrictions should be imposed by regulation or by persuasion? what distinctions should be made between media? whether there should be a tax on advertising? whether to urge the companies to switch their advertising towards pipes, cigars, filter tips - or to distinguish in any controls imposed between these different kinds of smoking? On under-age sales, the committee should consider the penalties, the case for wider powers, whether 16 was the right age, stronger powers over slot machines, more vigorous enforcement. They should end with a note of the situation in other countries, and a 'compendious statement' of existing laws.

The committee worked hard, with papers presented on topics as various as whether the licensing powers for cinemas could be adapted to require bans on smoking (they could not), whether vending machines should be banned (perhaps), whether smoking by customers in food shops should be banned (no: the reason for the existing ban on smoking by employees was the risk of transferring germs from the mouth to the hands and had nothing to do with the smoke or ash); and whether the minimum age for sale of tobacco should be raised to 18 (no point) or the fines for breach of the law increased (ineffective 'when detection is so uncertain'). The law restricting the sale of alcohol worked better partly because a licence was required and 'it would be possible to subject the sale of tobacco to a similar system of justices' licences, with consequent restrictions on the places at which and/or the hours during which it was sold; but that would be using a sledgehammer - and without any certainty of cracking the nut.'

The insurance industry was asked about differential premiums and replied that 'actuarially the risks are not really significant and do not warrant special treatment.' Besides, how could the companies monitor their policy-holders' non-smoking? Nor would the life assurance companies wish to publicise smoking risks among their clients, since 'these risks appear to be no greater than, if as great as, risks from many other practices, e.g., drinking, or eating fatty foods . . . ' and publicity could be counterproductive if it led to a demand for lower premiums and the companies had to reveal that smoking was not actuarially significant.

The committee had a meeting on 17 April with industry representatives who produced a draft circular to retailers urging vigilance against under-age sales but rejected action against vending machines. They argued against any further restriction on television advertising ('cigarette advertising was not especially directed to young persons: the 'romantic theme' had a strong appeal for the middle-aged and elderly') and urged the need for further research.

The Scottish Office again proposed a major public education campaign with a national steering committee comprising (among others) representatives of the BMA, the TUC and the Federation of British Industry, the church, youth and education and a budget of £1 million. The Central Office of Information proposed by contrast a £25,000 campaign using free rather than paid-for media, offering as reasons that otherwise 'the Government would be fighting a vast commercial interest on the least favourable ground' and that it was 'unwise to set a pace faster than can with certainty be maintained over a period of three years' while 'under the shadow of a threat of Government action or opposition, the cigarette manufacturers themselves may decide to modify their advertising approach - in particular its association with youth and romance . . .' Meantime, the Ministry of Health produced half a dozen posters to offer to local authorities providing, in accordance with Cabinet policy, facts rather than 'active discouragement'.

Behind the work of the interdepartmental committee lay the largely defensive and often extraordinarily amateurish preparations in individual departments. In the Board of Trade the Undersecretary G J MacMahon defined his department's interests as avoidance of 'unnecessary damage' to the industry; concern for tobacco-growing countries, especially in the Commonwealth, and concern for protection of the public as consumers of tobacco.[24] Selby-Boothroyd prepared a brief for MacMahon, picking up a discarded theory mentioned in the College report and elaborating it at length. Theorising as an 'informed layman' about people being divided into those ('soft-shells') vulnerable to lung cancer and ' "biologically self-protective" hard-shells', he ended four densely argued pages with the startling conclusion:

> The most the R.C.P. have shown is that cigarette smoking may be the cause of lung cancer, and that quite a lot of other things may equally be dangerous. It hardly seems sure enough ground on which to build a political platform.

His boss Miss K E Boyes, the Assistant Secretary, also found the report 'disappointing regarded as a scientific enquiry. Doctors,' she said, 'are by habit and training inclined to the pontifical in expressing their views' and had failed to learn that 'the conventional wisdom of the profession' had often proved wrong in the past. However, 'the Minister of Health has clearly swallowed the Report hook, line and sinker'.

A week later (22 March) she attended a briefing meeting for Lord Hailsham, who was to answer another debate in the House of Lords. She reported:

> It was clear that Lord Hailsham holds very strong personal views on the subject to which he intends to give free rein. In particular he is extremely critical of the tobacco companies for their replies to the R.C.P. Report; he says that these are deliberately dishonest and wicked from start to finish and that their authors are selling their fellow men for thirty pieces of silver.

Departmental representatives had been unhappy with his strong line and had tried in vain to moderate it, until, she wrote, she herself intervened to

> suggest that it might be found very useful at a later stage to have the co-operation of the industry in certain ways and that this would be more easily achieved if they had not been too heavily blackguarded first, and I think he may have taken this point.

According to her, Hailsham was dubious about controls on advertising but keen on promoting filter-tips, cigars and pipes despite doubts by 'Ministry of Health scientists' about the evidence on these supposedly safer forms of smoking.

The previous day she had been at a private Board of Trade meeting with Partridge and Todd, who clearly felt themselves amongst friends. They had developed the line set out in the industry's original statement by deploring the risk that a public education campaign could 'set up a powerful reaction by spreading nervous tension, especially between children and their (smoking) parents. "Create a cancer-phobia and you don't know what you're doing" ' - but the press and public might turn against the Government for it. As to controls on the themes used in advertising, a minority in the House of Commons were 'stirring up the latent Puritanism lingering in this country'. Clearly wearing his company rather than his industry hat, Partridge took a sideswipe at Gallaher for their 'objectionable' promotion by coupons of their Kensitas brand and at Carreras for their promotion of filter-tips, which might be no safer than untipped cigarettes: Imperial had no coupon-promoted brand and only a toe-hold in the filter-tip market.[25]

The Carreras group (which evolved into Rothmans and is now part of BAT) moved quickly to exploit this advantage. On 5 April its chairman, R W S Plumley, wrote to the President of the Board of Trade, Frederick Erroll, with a copy of a carefully crafted public statement from his company on smoking and health. Declining as tobacco manufacturers to take issue with the Royal College of Physicians' report ('which is based mainly upon the collection and collation of statistical data') it called for the subject to be 'kept in perspective and considered positively and constructively. . . Over indulgence in any pleasure could always be harmful: moderation in all things is a good maxim.'

The statement then developed a theme of safer smoking. The Government, which received £800 million in tax each year, should cooperate with the industry in a major research project. The College report had mentioned the possibility of filters reducing the harmful effects of smoking, and Carreras would be concentrating even more fully on these in future. Longer stub lengths were possibly safer - but high tax told against discarding unsmoked tobacco, although again filters would help. As to children, Carreras would be removing all its vending machines from streets and public places and confining its television advertising to hours when children were least likely to be viewing.

Carreras, as the *Financial Times* reported, had not consulted the TMSC before making its own statement. Its démarche forced an 'emergency meeting' of Imperial, Gallaher and three smaller companies, after which they announced that they too would limit television advertising to after 9.00 p.m. Carreras followed up this coup with persistent lobbying over many months of the Lord President, the Minister of Health and the Chancellor of the Exchequer, pressing the virtues of its filter technology and seeking Government collaboration with the industry on research.[26]

The Board of Trade now clashed with the Ministry of Health over responsibility for any putative controls on tobacco advertising. Colonel Sir Leonard Ropner, Conservative MP for Barkston Ash, had put down a Parliamentary Question on the subject for the Home Office. Health, Trade and the Home Office were all clear it was not a Home Office responsibility, but in the end Butler had to answer the question as both Health and Trade vigorously asserted it was the responsibility of the other. Butler wrote to Erroll on 29 March with a copy to Powell asking them to settle the matter, and eventually on 27 April Sir Bruce Fraser advised Powell 'I am disposed to modify my previous view that the Board of Trade's attitude was wholly unreasonable.'

In the Ministry of Health the Public Relations Division paid close attention to a junior official's report of the views of a single (if intelligent) schoolgirl, and the Division formed an Advisory Group on Publicity comprising headteachers and officers from local health and education authorities as well as Whitehall representatives.[27] On 21 March, local health authorities were invited to put in orders for the first three Ministry posters - eight were being prepared, along with a leaflet, a one-reel film and a filmstrip. These conformed with Cabinet policy in offering facts rather than 'active discouragement'.[28] Enoch Powell received a list of this material bearing the manuscript annotation: 'The 'skull' poster isn't mentioned'. He wrote on it: 'I agree. I think there should be an early H (horror) series e.g., the skull, the skeleton hand with the match, the two diseased lungs etc.'

A letter from Sir Hugh Lucas-Tooth, Conservative MP for Hendon South, asking whether there was any danger to 'those who are subjected to the smoke of others in confined spaces' was referred for advice to Dr Charles Fletcher, the secretary of the College's committee, who replied that the matter of other people's smoke was not dealt with in the report because of 'the impossibility of obtaining valid epidemiological evidence'. He suggested, however, that asthma might result from such exposure, and a reply to this effect was in due course sent.[29]

Elsewhere in Whitehall, the Central Office of Information commissioned a consultant to advise on publicity (the key point in his report was that 'A clarification of what the Government wishes to accomplish immediately and in the long-term must precede the preparation of a detailed publicity plan' but the emphasis of his proposals was on 'safer' smoking)[30]; the Admiralty prepared a report on stopping the sale of tax-free cigarettes to servicemen and a Royal Army Medical Corps survey found that young soldiers had started smoking on average at age 16.

The General Post Office became involved on several fronts. They sought advice on a postal franking slogan referred to them as potentially controversial by the plate maker from which it had been ordered by Basildon Urban District Council: *'Cancer! Protect your Health - Increase your Wealth - Stop Smoking'*. Mrs O'Brien at the Ministry of Health advised her boss: 'While we can steer a course between making the facts known and active discouragement this is not a distinction which officials would care to have to expound to a local authority' and suggested that no objection be raised.[31]

The GPO was unreceptive to anti-smoking advertising in post offices: their public relations department wrote to Heald:

> Our position is that we do not display advertisements on matters which can be taken to be controversial . . . I should add of course that we are refusing to accept anti-smoking slogans in other advertising space but the posters you could wish to display would presumably be put up on the noticeboards reserved for other Government departments.[32]

The GPO was also concerned about television advertising, which became a focus of increasing attention over the next two years. Miss Mervyn Pike, Assistant Postmaster-General, told the Commons on 13 March that the matter was being looked at 'with the greatest urgency' and the GPO had indeed by then sought advice from the Board of Trade, saying that they currently took the view that it was 'inappropriate to prohibit or control advertisements for tobacco and cigarettes on television alone, while leaving other forms of advertising completely free'. Already by agreement between the Independent Television Authority and the television companies no tobacco advertisements were shown during or around children's programmes, and following a statement in the Commons in January by the Postmaster General the ITA was implementing a ban on such advertisements between 5 p.m. and 7 p.m. (This was before the industry volunteered its 9.00 p.m. threshold.) Under the Television Act the ITA had a duty to comply with the recommendations of its Advertising Advisory Committee, on which Ministry of Health was represented, but the Committee was unlikely to ban or restrict tobacco advertising without guidance or direction from the Government. With the Pilkington Committee on broadcasting policy about to report, the PMG thought it impolitic to exercise the powers under the Act which would allow him to ban tobacco advertising (but did not allow him to limit the hours in which it appeared); he could, however, probably 'prohibit the 'romantic' type of advertising cigarettes which might be considered a special inducement to young people'. The Board of Trade reacted negatively to the idea of further controls, noting that consumption had not risen in line with increased advertising expenditure, that the press and the advertising profession would oppose a ban and that the tobacco industry would protest if drink advertising was not similarly penalised.[33]

Notes

1. Personal communication, 19 January 1998: Sir George comments: 'Enoch Powell was a strong Minister with whom I had good report but I could not persuade him to ban cigarette advertising for the same reason as Virginia Bottomley gave later: "commercial freedom of speech".'

2. PRO file MH 55.2227

3. PRO files MH 55.2204, BT 258.200. The Board of Trade file has a cutting from the *Financial Times* (8 December 1961) pointing out that only foreign manufacturers would be affected by the ban 'since under pressure from the anti-smoke (sic) faction in Parliament, the Italian State tobacco monopoly has in recent years been forced to refrain from advertising its products'. The ban, which passed its final stages on April 5, was in the event virtually unenforced, the fines for its breach being negligible.

4. BMJ 1961; **ii**: 1625, 16 December 1961. The Swedish precedent was a weak one: according to a Ministry of Health paper (GEN 763/6, 30 March 1962) based on information from the Royal College of Physicians, 'in 1956 there was a temporary stop to advertising by the Swedish tobacco monopoly' - PRO file CAB 130.185.

5.   PRO file MH 55.2226

6.   PRO file BT 258.200

7.   PRO file T 171.593. See also chapter 5, note 2.

8.   PRO file MH 55.2204

9.   Paper HA(62)21 - PRO file CAB 134:1990. The paper - and the subsequent Cabinet paper - quoted the Report's conclusions at length and set out in full the recommendations for Government action:

> '(i)   more education of the public and especially schoolchildren concerning the hazards of smoking;
>
> '(ii)   more effective restrictions on the sale of tobacco to children;
>
> '(iii) restriction of tobacco advertising;
>
> '(iv) wider restriction of smoking in public places;
>
> '(v)   an increase of tax on cigarettes, perhaps with adjustment of the tax on pipe and cigar tobaccos;
>
> '(vi) informing purchasers of the tar and nicotine content of the smoke of cigarettes;
>
> '(vii) investigating the value of anti-smoking clinics to help those who find difficulty in giving up smoking.'

10.   Paper C(62)43 - PRO file CAB 129:108.

11.   Cabinet minutes CC.19(62) item 4 and CC.20(62) item 2. The circulars were issued on 12 March. Circular 6/62 from the Ministry of Health said 'health education should increasingly emphasise the hazards of smoking' and called on health authorities to 'bring home to the public the dangers . . . of smoking', promising free publicity material. Circular 3/62 from the Ministry of Education called for a 'fresh and positive effort . . . to discourage smoking among children' and expressed the hope that staff would not smoke 'anywhere in school in front of children.' - PRO files MH 55.2204 and MH 55.2233.

12.   PRO files MH 55.2227, MH 55.2237

13.   Minute, 1 March 1962, by Miss K E Boyes, Assistant Secretary, Industries and Manufactures Department, who made the point that she was a non-smoker - PRO file BT 258.200.

14.   An assessment of Todd's paper was made for the Chief Medical Officer by his medical staff. Their conclusion was that 'a very clever defence is made for the Tobacco Manufacturers. There is no denial of the almost certain relationship between smoking and cancer of the lung although all possible is done to confuse the issue.' In their detailed analysis they said, *à propos* air pollution: 'Here, Mr Todd makes points which range from good ones to others which are verging on the dishonest.' They agreed that much of the research he recommended was worth undertaking - PRO file MH 55.2232.

15.   PRO file MH 55.2233

16.   PRO file MH 55.2204

17.   PRO file MH 55.2234

18.   Robinson three years later as Minister of Health carried the ban on television
       cigarette advertising through Cabinet.

19.   PRO file MH 154.182

20.   PRO file MH 55.2204

21.   PRO files BT 258.200, BT 258.201

22.   PRO file CAB 124.1673

23.   Its official title was GEN 763 and all its papers and minutes are to be found
       on PRO file CAB 130.185.

24.   MacMahon was the Board of Trade representative on the interdepartmental
       committee - PRO file BT 258.1405. Another undersecretary, G Bowen, wrote
       later in the month 'our responsibility is to see that the views of the industry
       are properly considered and taken account of; it is not however necessary for
       us to endorse them' - PRO file BT 258.201.

25.   PRO file BT 258.200

26.   The full story is perhaps worth telling. The Carreras Managing Director,
       R W S Plumley, sent Hailsham a copy of his company's statement. Hailsham
       replied:

> I am glad that, like me, you feel unable to challenge the Report
> of the Royal College of Physicians and that at least some of the
> suggestions I made in my speech [i.e., in House of Lords, 22
> March 1962] seem to be acceptable to you. For your
> information, however, the Government does not earmark
> money for particular projects of medical research. This is the
> function of the Medical Research Council who make their
> decisions on the scientific merits of the particular projects
> submitted to them. This usually depends on the extent to
> which particular leads appear promising and the availability of
> manpower of suitable quality. Lung cancer is a sufficiently
> serious disease to make research into it which satisfies these
> criteria justifiable independently of the revenue derived from
> cigarette smoking. This is not intrinsically - although the
> prevalence of cigarette smoking to which it is related probably
> is - a matter the Medical Research Council would be likely to
> consider relevant.

Plumley replied reiterating that Parliament and the public wished to be reassured that 'no effort will be spared to find out what, if any, are the harmful elements in cigarette smoke' and to remove them:

> It is for this reason that we stated our belief that the industry and the Government should co-operate in a major research project and that the Government may feel it has an obligation to increase the amount of grants towards such research.

Hailsham's private secretary replied that Hailsham did not dispute the need for research, but 'the statistical evidence which had been deployed was so strong that it could not be ignored whilst further research was proceeding' and that no promising proposals for research had been rejected for lack of funds.

Plumley then requested a meeting with Hailsham. The Board of Trade briefed his office that while it was quite appropriate for Hailsham as Minister of Science to see representatives of the industry to discuss research, Carreras had only about 5% of the market and were members of the Tobacco Manufacturers' Standing Committee: 'Mr Plumley has the reputation of wanting to draw attention to himself and could not be regarded as representative of the industry.' Hailsham, asked by his office if they should arrange a meeting, replied: 'Yes, but give me some nasty things to say to him and in particular let me have copies of some Carreras advertisements of cigarettes.'

So briefed, he met Plumley on 15 June. Plumley tried to make a case for joint research; Hailsham politely but firmly rebuffed him: 'He reaffirmed that research into cancer was not held up by shortage of funds. If good men came forward with promising ideas for research their proposals would be considered very sympathetically. Money spent on research by first class men was rarely wasted even if the particular line of research did not in the end turn out to be fruitful; on the other hand money spent on second rate men with second rate ideas, would be a waste. The Lord President doubted whether a formal joint council between Government and industry was the right way of securing co-ordination in research' and suggested that Plumley keep in touch with the Medical Research Council. Plumley wrote thanking Hailsham for the meeting: 'It was also very kind of you to say that I may call upon you again in connection with this subject when I may have anything further to add to my remarks and I shall have great pleasure in so doing.'

Meantime, he had already asked for a meeting with Enoch Powell: 'You may remember we last met at a luncheon given by N M Rothschild and Sons, New Court. . . I should very much like an opportunity of a discussion with you at a time and date that may be convenient to you. I believe that such a discussion could be useful as we are naturally concerned with the further examination of the matter and research development.' The Ministry, aware of the impending meeting with Hailsham, replied asking what points Plumley wished to make. Plumley replied in somewhat general terms but indicating that the key issue was filter cigarettes. At this point MacMahon from the

Board of Trade reported a meeting a week earlier with Plumley's Assistant Managing Director, C A C Bulpitt, at which he had talked excitedly about American research suggesting that the harmful element in cigarette smoke was 'a phenolic compound' and claiming that Carreras' filters would be able to remove 85% of the phenols from tobacco smoke. Bulpitt had already discussed the theory - based on research (MacMahon had found out by the next day) by Dr E L Wynder - with Sir Robert Platt, the President of the Royal College of Physicians, and Charles Fletcher. Powell's office then declined the suggestion of a meeting on the grounds that the point on joint research had been covered by Hailsham and that on other points 'the Minister has no views beyond those in the Report of the Royal College, which he accepts.'

Plumley tried again in October: he wrote to Hailsham seeking 'a few moments' with him. It was discovered that Plumley had made no approach to the Medical Research Council, despite agreeing to do so after his first meeting with Hailsham, but then it was revealed that the point of concern now was brand promotion by gift coupons, a point of contention between the companies.

Then on 17 October Plumley, accompanied by one Michael Rice, had a meeting with the Chancellor of the Exchequer, Reginald Maudling. Miss Boyes of the Board of Trade prepared a brief, leaving a comment on her own file: 'It was not clear to me why the Chancellor should be having a general discussion about the tobacco industry but it appears that Mr Michael Rice is a personal friend of the Chancellor and has obtained the entrée for Mr Plumley as he did on one or two occasions when Mr Maudling was at the Board of Trade . . .'

Maudling wrote his own note of his meeting:

> They were interested in two points - the effect of the Common Market on tobacco duty, and the re-emergence of gift coupons and cigarette cards.
>
> On the first point, I told them that my impression was that nothing in the Treaty of Rome forced us to revise our method of charging tobacco duty . . .
>
> On the second point, I explained that . . . the Government were unlikely to take any action. He made the point that at the Government's request the tobacco companies were not appealing to young people in their advertising. Would it not be inconsistent with this if, for example, a company came out with a line of cigarette cards designed to have such an appeal? I said I would mention this to Lord Hailsham, who I gather had conducted the talks with the industry, but I did not undertake to do anything further.

Hailsham then wrote to Plumley declining a further meeting in view of the meetings already held with him, adding:

> You will be interested, and I hope amused, to learn that
> someone in your organisation sent me a small box of your
> filter tipped Piccadilly and asked me to try them. This was
> indeed bearding the lion in his den, but it was as ineffectual as
> the devil's attempt on St Anthony.

- PRO files CAB 124.1674, MH 55.2234, BT 258.201.

Carreras continued to press their advantage in filter-tips: in January 1964,
Plumley wrote at length to Reginald Maudling, the Chancellor of the
Exchequer, enclosing a copy of a very mildly encouraging letter the US
Surgeon-General, Luther Terry, had sent to a US Senator. Maudling passed
copies to the Minister of Health (by then Anthony Barber) and others and
sent a bland acknowledgement - PRO file BT 258.202.

27.   The members of the Group met on 4 April and many subsequently submitted
personal memoranda. A summary was prepared for the interdepartmental
working party. On 10 April the Secretary of the Association of Municipal
Corporations wrote objecting to that the Ministry had approached 'people
in the employment of local authorities' without going through the Association
which represented them - PRO files MH 55.2204, MH 55.2237.

28.   Paper GEN 763/5, PRO files CAB 130.185, MH 55.2233. The Central
Council for Health Education was preparing other material. A headline in the
Sunday Times on 8 April said: 'Campaign Against Smoking Too Feeble Say
Councils' - the cutting is on a Board of Trade file, BT 258.201. On 17 May
Dame Enid Russell-Smith minuted Sir Bruce Fraser with news of a private
initiative in anti-smoking publicity:

> On a lighter note, the Minister will have noticed the anti-
> smoking posters which have been carried up and down Regent
> Street on sandwich boards every evening for the past fortnight
> by a group of young people. When stopping to look at the
> posters I have twice been asked if I wanted help and have been
> given literature. This directed attention to two anti-smoking
> films being shown at the New Gallery where a Harley Street
> medical man would be in attendance to give help to those who
> needed it. I was a little startled to find that the organisation
> behind this activity was the Seventh Day Adventists but am
> sorry I have not found time to see the films* or consult the
> Harley Street specialist.

> * Mr Heald thought them quite good.

- PRO file MH 55.2234. The Seventh Day Adventists have remained
significant anti-smoking campaigners to this day, although not in the United
Kingdom.

29.   Ministry Medical Officers exchanged views on the file at the end of May about

the effects of passive smoking, agreeing (in the words of Dr A Cruickshank) that 'Whilst we do not know that inhalation of other people's smoke is a physical risk to healthy people we cannot say definitely that it does not constitute one, and it may be the factor which sets off an adolescent on his smoking career or in causing someone who has recently stopped to restart.' PRO file MH 55.2234.

30.   *The Role of Publicity in the Smoking and Health Campaign*, by Anthony Hyde of Armstrong Warden Ltd, April 1962 - PRO file MH 55.2237.

31.   This was not the end of problems with franking slogans. When the officials' report was being considered by Lord Hailsham's Ministerial Committee the Assistant Postmaster-General, Miss Mervyn Pike, without notice explained her worries and got an agreement that 'the Post Office would continue to resist, as far as was practicable, requests from public health authorities for permission to frank letters with anti-smoking slogans' because such slogans were 'controversial and not permissible under the Post Office's normal practice'. The Ministry of Health, ambushed, persuaded the Committee at its next meeting to require the Post Office to consult them. However, even the Ministry of Health were equivocal about the Basildon slogan: 'there remains the point whether the word "stop" in the slogan is good psychology' but the Ministry was leaving local authorities to do the publicity and - suggested J P Dodds - should not interfere. The Public Relations head S A Heald disagreed: 'While agreeing with Mr Dodds that it is difficult to read a lesson to a local authority on publicity techniques, I do feel that they should be persuaded not to use the "stop smoking" line. (The G.P.O. incidentally mentioned that there was a tobacco firm in the district.) Could we not say (without too much risk of being misunderstood) that at the present stage of the campaign we are concerned with persuasion leading to conviction borne of an appreciation of the facts and that the exhortation to "stop smoking" should be reserved for a later stage? Used at the present juncture it is felt that it might invoke "resistance" and, therefore, prejudice the main lines on which the long-term campaign is at present being developed.' Dodds noted on his copy: 'I gather the Dep. Secretary is agreeing to Mr Heald trying to convert Basildon' but the outcome is not revealed on the file - PRO file MH 55.2234. See also below on page 125.

32.   PRO file MH 55.2204

33.   PRO file BT 258:1405

5

1962:
The End of the Beginning

The committee of officials - known as GEN 763 - produced its report on 15 May 1962. It dealt in order with the recommendations made by the Royal College of Physicians. The officials were clear that it was impossible to sustain the separation between dissuading children from smoking and merely presenting adults with the facts, but they were against the sort of mass media campaign the Scottish Office had long favoured:

> If the Government were to spend very large sums of public money on a mass campaign, consideration would have to be given to the restriction of advertising by the tobacco companies. A publicity campaign of this kind would cost at least £1 million a year and the tobacco companies are at present spending £11 million a year. If the Government decide that as a matter of policy action must be taken to discourage smoking, launch an extensive advertising campaign but leave tobacco advertising untouched, it would be difficult to justify to public opinion what would be bound to appear as a conflict between Government policy and the tobacco companies. To restrict tobacco advertising would require legislation . . . If the Government embarked on a competitive advertising campaign, it would be difficult to withdraw if the results did not match up to expectation . . .

If the possibility of a mass campaign were kept in reserve, however, 'the tobacco companies might voluntarily restrict the scale and modify the content of their own publicity'. The Committee recommended therefore a campaign using the available authoritative and opinion-forming channels and free media, planned over a period initially of three years by a steering committee with representatives from all relevant departments and at a cost of about £50,000 a year exclusive of staff. They added that the BBC and ITA might be asked to co-operate.

> But any publicity campaign, however well planned, is in our view unlikely to have any lasting effect by itself on smoking habits. Past investigations seem to show that smokers will not be inclined to change their habits unless they not only accept the link between smoking and lung cancer, but believe that the reality of the risk is accepted by the Government in its actions as well as in its publicity. [There was therefore a need for] other forms of action, which apart from any direct deterrent effect would reinforce the propaganda. Moreover, if the object of public education is to produce a reduction in smoking, a campaign on the dangers of smoking must be accompanied by some reduction in present propaganda in favour of smoking, either by direct Government action or by voluntary restrictions imposed by the owners of publicity media - the Press, ITV and poster firms, or by the tobacco manufacturers.

The Committee considered and rejected a tax on advertising, stated without argument: 'It would seem unreasonable to ban tobacco advertising . . . on ITV while allowing it to continue unrestricted in the Press and on hoardings', but noted that the ITA was convinced of the need for changes in the themes of television advertising. However, for the Government to determine a permitted level of advertising would be 'an invidious task', while a total ban would lead to pressure on the Government to treat in the same way liquor and other advertising of commodities 'whose immoderate use presents a danger to health'. Voluntary measures by the advertising media and by the tobacco industry were therefore preferable to legislative action by the Government. 'We believe that the most hopeful course of action at present would be to keep the threat of legislation in reserve, to impress on the responsible authorities the seriousness with which the Government regard the dangers of cigarette smoking, to invite their co-operation and to await results.'

On under-age sales, the Committee concluded that although the law was 'easily evaded . . . it would not be reasonable to expect stricter control'. Penalties should be increased (the fine for a first offence was only £2), but as a political rather than a practical gesture (this was done by a backbench amendment to the Children and Young Persons Act in 1963). They rejected any advance in the minimum age for sale to 17 or 18, controls on vending machines in public places, banning sales of fewer than ten cigarettes, and (sensibly) making it an offence for a child to smoke. They considered at some length a system of justices' licences to sell tobacco, which could be revoked if a retailer were convicted of under-age sales but said it would produce substantial administrative work and enforcement problems for very small advantages. In the end the only recommendation they made was that Customs and Excise should agree to the request from the tobacco companies to help with the circulation of a notice to all retailers protesting their concern at sales to children. (It went out about 25 June.[1])

The National Society of Non-Smokers had been pressing for controls on smoking in public places, and the Committee considered half-heartedly a number of possible restrictions. Tobacco smoke was not held to be injurious to non-smokers but restrictions 'might help to make the public aware of the dangers of smoking'. However, enforcement of any legislation would be difficult and 'effective action will be possible only when there has been a significant change in the public attitude to smoking.'

Similarly they saw no future for use of taxation to discourage smoking:

> An increase in tobacco duty would have to be very substantial to be likely to produce a cut in consumption. The lower social classes (who tend to be the heaviest smokers) would be heavily penalised; at any rate in the initial stages, the cost of living index would rise and wage claims would be stimulated; and the large reduction in our tobacco imports would have a serious effect on the economies of some of the exporting countries, notably Rhodesia.

(This last argument of course is an objection to any step that might be effective in reducing consumption.) Moreover, the Committee continued, differentially high taxation of cigarettes compared with other tobacco would present

> formidable problems of definition and administration. The differential could readily be evaded by home production of cigarettes from pipe tobacco, even if it were found practicable to prevent the 400,000 retail tobacconists from producing cigarettes in the same way for sale.

They rejected the Royal College of Physicians' inadequately considered recommendation about putting tar and nicotine yields on packets: the College had admitted there was 'no scientific reason behind their recommendation' and it might encourage a false sense of security: the tobacco companies would 'contrive to imply' that lower yields were safer which was not known to be true. (Here the Committee in their anxiety to find justification for inaction stumbled, it would seem, on a half-truth they are unlikely to have believed at the time.)

The officials ended their report by recording their exchanges with the insurance industry and noting that the Ministry of Health would be encouraging local authorities and hospitals 'to set up a small number of experimental anti-smoking clinics' with a review of results in two years' time.

The committee's report was considered by Lord Hailsham's Ministerial Committee on Smoking and Health on 21 May, 1 and 26 June. Broadly speaking, they accepted the officials' recommendations. They agreed at last that 'no attempt should be made to confine publicity directed at adults to purely factual material, if only because it would be found impracticable to distinguish between what was factual and what was persuasive.' They also wanted it to be 'made clear that quick results could not be expected even from a major publicity campaign and that a continuing and long-term campaign was contemplated.'

Ministers were more enthusiastic than the officials about discouraging smoking in public places - they noted that it was 'not entirely harmless to other persons present: coughing and asthma brought on by smoke could be harmful to persons with heart complaints' - and they thought the public would be receptive to controls introduced on public transport, in shops and other places. Such action should be positively encouraged.

They commissioned further consideration of retailer licensing as a way to control under-age sales.[2] The committee of officials responded with a paper urging the huge difficulties of definition and enforcement in any system that sought to ban offenders from selling tobacco - a 'draconian' penalty. Ministers bowed before the length and complexity rather than the cogency of the arguments.

They were also uneasy about rejecting increased taxation as a way of discouraging smoking. A new paper on the subject was commissioned from Anthony Barber, the Economic Secretary to the Treasury, who argued at length the case against switching from a system of taxation of all tobacco by weight of leaf to one that dealt separately with different products. There were policy objections to the change, which would have to be designed either 'to effect a significant change in smoking habits' or else 'as a gesture'. A gesture would soon be seen through, while to affect consumption significantly a price increase of 50-100% would be required: 'There is no product for which the demand has remained so resilient under increased taxation.' This 'would lead to considerable avoidance of duty . . . would be thought to be unfair' because of the effect on the poor and on women, who could not switch to pipes or cigars, 'would be politically unpopular' and 'although there may be no 'principle of taxation' involved, would be thought by most cigarette smokers to be a wrong use of taxation'. Ministers remained split on the issue and decided to report their differences to the Cabinet.

The Cabinet considered the Ministerial Committee's report on 12 July and was less than enthusiastic. Ministers grudgingly approved the proposed publicity campaign ('inappropriate to consider at the present stage action on a wider front or more drastic in character'), decided it would be 'preferable that the Government should not intervene' in discouraging smoking in public places, and recorded no discussion at all on any other question, including tax.[3]

Notes on Board of Trade files later in the year state plainly what can easily be read between the lines of the minutes: 'My impression,' wrote Miss K E Boyes,

> when the Cabinet considered the Ministerial Report last July, was that, with the exception of Lord Hailsham, Ministers, and especially the P.M., were pretty firmly agreed that they were not anxious to stick their fingers into this very difficult pie save to the limited extent of giving the 'all clear' for the health and education campaign. The Prime Minister, in particular, was reported by Mr M Cary [Cabinet Office] to have said that he did not propose to contemplate any further action, not even the statement which he had earlier more or less promised . . .'

and her boss G J MacMahon wrote to the Second Secretary, Sir Leslie Robinson:

> The Cabinet were less inclined to dramatic action than either the Lord President or the Minister of Health. The general view was that it would be inappropriate to consider at the present stage action on a wider front or more drastic in character than the 'free publicity' campaign recommended by the Committee of Ministers. The Prime Minister was not at all keen to make a statement in Parliament and it was left that the Lord President, in consultation with the other Ministers concerned, would prepare a draft statement for his consideration. . . '[4]

A draft statement was put to the Ministerial Committee on 25 July: it said the Government accepted a duty to see that the evidence was 'set clearly before the public, particularly the young' by means of a campaign, 'extended over a number of years':

> It is now proposed to make the facts about smoking available to a wide range of the media of public information, including the Press, radio and television. The Government intend to provide material and notes for speakers and will distribute other publicity to Post Offices, Government Establishments, doctors, churches, youth clubs and similar organisations. All these groups will be invited to co-operate with the Departments concerned in planning the details of the campaign and in maintaining its momentum.

But Hailsham had already been briefed by Cary that 'the Prime Minister plainly does not wish to make the statement himself'[5] and in the Ministerial Committee

> discussion showed it to be the general view of the Committee that no statement should be made in Parliament on this subject before the summer recess. The Health Ministers were not under any pressure to make a statement and, on matters within their Departmental responsibility, could add little to what they had already said . . .

Hailsham wrote to the Prime Minister:

> Parliamentary interest in the subject seems for the moment to have abated and a statement might well have the effect of stimulating it. This would not matter if we had a more powerful case to present, but as things stand it could be embarrassing. The announcement of our modest publicity campaign will give little satisfaction to those who believe that we ought to take stronger measures, and unfavourable comment before the campaign has even started would tend to reduce its effectiveness still further; in the light of the Cabinet's decisions there are no other steps which we can announce or for which we can take credit.

> I propose, therefore, that the machinery for the publicity campaign should be set up and that the campaign itself should be launched without any accompanying statement in Parliament of our intentions to do so. Later in the year, when the campaign has perhaps achieved some modest success, it might be useful to make a statement claiming credit for it. This can wait upon events.

Macmillan, in the words of MacMahon of the Board of Trade later in the year, 'accepted [the recommendation] with alacrity.' He wrote on the memorandum: 'I feel sure that this is the best thing to do. No statement. H.M.'[6]

Hailsham and Powell nevertheless managed to maintain a campaign on smoking. In the Ministry of Health, Dr Godber began to find out how little information was available about helping people stop smoking. A paper to the Medical and Mental Health Standing Advisory Committees in May 1962 had news of two clinics in Britain - one in Salford run for the National Society of Non-Smokers by Dr J L Burn, the other at the Central Middlesex chest clinic - and of 14-day courses of interviews, injections and tablets in Sweden. 'Immediate results are reported to be good, but the relapse rate, it is suspected, is considerable.' The two committees met on 5 June and heard that the Maudsley Hospital was considering starting a clinic. It was proposed that the MRC might conduct research on the psychology of motivation to stop and that a conference be held to bring together all those with experience in the field. Godber wrote the next day to Sir Harold Himsworth at the MRC passing on a suggestion from Dr Dennis Hill that such research might be based on asking the doctors in the Bradford Hill/Doll study who had stopped smoking how and why they had done so. Sir Harold replied on 20 June that this appeared 'a tall order' and suggested lunch. Nothing appears to have come of the proposal.

A conference was held, however, on 27 July, at which the relevant doctors reported on the clinics in Salford, at the Central Middlesex and in Huddersfield (where the Medical Officer of Health reported 70-90 people attending his clinic in its first three weeks). Dr Horace Joules, making a final appearance on the files, reported on the Swedish clinics - but his report was omitted from the final version of the minutes. On 27 September, the CMO sent out a circular to local health authorities enclosing these final minutes and saying: 'The Minister would like to see a few more clinics started up as soon as possible. Can you . . . consider the possibilities in your Region?'

Reports from clinics were then gathered and practical ideas were exchanged and circulated. A report from Salford mentioned sessions of an hour a week for about six weeks (or as long as individuals wished to come) for 'elementary group therapy'. Aids were systematically listed: chewing or sucking edible/non-edible material; using tobacco substitutes (e.g., menthol crystals in a cigarette-holder); sipping water; lengthening the intervals between cigarettes; public declarations of intention; saving up the money that would have been spent on tobacco; avoiding the company of smokers. There was also mention of a duplicated sheet of breathing exercises. In 1963 preliminary results were reported from a Smokers' Advisory Clinic for staff of the Ministry of Health. After seven weeks, nine out of 19 men and one of 12 women had stopped smoking and the rest had reduced their consumption by various amounts. The Board of Trade copy is annotated in inaccurate mockery: '30 people out of how many in the Ministry of Health? And over what period of time? And nearly half reverted to their addiction! NINE souls saved. Is this not great nonsense?'[7]

Steps were taken also to formalise the publicity campaign against smoking. A steering group was instituted to co-ordinate the campaign - but not to initiate or execute it, responsibilities which were retained by the Health departments. Dame Enid Russell-Smith wrote that it was 'essential that there should be at least one woman member' and proposed that the TUC be asked to nominate one because that would also bring in the 'industrial population' and help persuade them that it is ' 'non-U' to smoke'. In the event, however, when the Ministerial Committee was asked to decide 'whether there should be a 'statutory housewife' or a T.U.C. representative' they rejected both - and pleased the Board of Trade, who wanted no part in work against their sponsored industry, by leaving them out as well.[8] Representation included the local authority associations, the BMA and Royal College of Physicians, Ministry of Education, Central Office of Information and others.

It is clear from its minutes that the Health Education Coordinating Committee lacked any influence. Dodds wrote from the Ministry of Health to Cary, the chairman of the officials' committee, on 18 January 1963 to say that at a meeting of the Coordinating Committee Charles Fletcher 'had quite a lot to say to the effect that the Government were not taking the matter seriously and had done very little' and had won agreement to quarterly reports on Government activity 'outside its purely health education activities. . . We shall have to scratch together whatever we can. But it isn't going to amount to a lot, and I have no hope that Dr Fletcher will be content.' Dodds copied his letter to other government departments to warn them of the 'pressure for energetic action' and the likelihood of 'public criticism'.[9]

The campaign ran into trouble with its posters. The *WPN and Advertisers Review* reported on 7 December that the Joint Censorship Committee of the outdoor poster industry has banned two Ministry of Health posters. One showed a cigarette with the words: 'Cancer - cigarettes cause lung cancer'; the other showed a rolled-up pound note burning like a cigarette, with the words: 'Smoking is an expensive way of damaging your health - cigarettes cause lung cancer'. Lord Francis-Williams raised the matter in the House of Lords. The Censorship Committee's secretary, H H Mallatratt, wrote to the Government with a brief:

> The Committee has . . . recently banned three posters issued by the Ministry of Health concerning lung cancer. These all contained the statement that 'cigarettes cause lung cancer'. This is, in the opinion of my Committee, undue exaggeration. They appreciate that a great deal of evidence has been adduced to show there is a link between lung cancer and smoking but they are not aware that there is positive proof that cigarettes do cause lung cancer. They would be perfectly willing to display, as they have done in the past, posters stating that cigarettes may cause lung cancer, and naturally they would reconsider their recent decisions if and when positive evidence is forthcoming to substantiate the wording of the rejected posters. Here again, I must point out that no outside pressure of any kind has been brought to bear to influence my Committee in its decision.

He quoted the Committee's terms of reference, which extended only to sites owned or controlled by members of subscribing associations. They included a power to ban posters that could 'be regarded as holding out for the prevention, cure or relief of serious diseases which should be rightly under the care of a registered medical practitioner . . .' The ineffable Selby-Boothroyd annotated the Board of Trade file: 'This covers it - and sums up the objection. The public are being urged: 'Don't smoke and you won't get lung cancer'. There is no proof of this.'

Lord Hailsham, who dealt with the matter in the Lords, replied trenchantly to Mallatratt. He accused his Committee of 'knowingly prevent[ing] the Minister of Health from communicating the findings of scientific opinion to the public', asked what qualifications his Committee had to assess scientific evidence and reach the decision that positive proof of smoking causing cancer was lacking, quoted the authorities that upheld that view and accused the Committee of a 'grave public disservice'.[10] Mallatratt replied, refusing to back down on his claim that 'Cigarettes cause lung cancer' went beyond anything the Ministry or the Royal College had said: a poster saying 'Cigarette smoking is a cause of lung cancer' would by the same token be acceptable.

Hailsham, irritated, sent a temporising reply, and a meeting was arranged between representatives of the Censorship Committee and Ministry of Health officials on 30 January 1963. Dodds, the Ministry undersecretary, wrote to Mallatratt on 15 February asking them to reconsider their position, whereby 'Cigarettes cause lung cancer' was a gross exaggeration but 'Cigarettes are a cause of lung cancer' was quite acceptable. The Committee replied in mid-March, holding to its position. Hailsham wrote a further letter accusing the Committee of 'taking responsibility on itself in a scientific matter on which every scientifically qualified body of any substance takes a contrary view'. The correspondence was then published in an answer to a question arranged in the House of Lords, with Hailsham condemning the Committee's 'absolutely indefensible and indeed irresponsible illogical quibbling'.[11]

However, the poster campaign continued, as did a travelling exhibition based on 'mobile units'. An assessment of their usefulness made in 1964 shows that two vans (later three) were operated by the Central Council for Health Education and were equipped to take films and lecturers to venues round the country, mainly to schools. They were functioning from the later months of 1962. The file is made up largely of correspondence about practical matters (schedules, expense accounts, problems with the vans) but includes a few assessments of the lecturers and the film. There is a general theme that, although the film was effective - its images of cancerous lungs were particularly mentioned - the lecturers were not dynamic or expert enough.

> The manner of presentation was not always convinced. A 'couldn't care less' approach or a flippant phrase will undermine the entire argument . . . I do not think the team's approach is professional enough - *City Health Department, Canterbury*

> The talks could have been 'put-over' with more energy and urgency - *Bradford school head*

> The lecturers were rather youthful and somewhat inexperienced - *another Bradford school head.*[12]

Enoch Powell quixotically devoted some energy during his last year as Minister to pursuing confectionery manufacturers who made sweet cigarettes for children.   He sent the packaging from one such product to his undersecretary J P Dodds in October 1962 and suggested an approach to the manufacturers. Amid official scepticism, the matter was referred to Lord Newton, the Parliamentary Secretary in the House of Lords, who suggested that sweet makers would gain by a decline in smoking and that an approach was worth trying. The approach was made through the Ministry of Agriculture,

Fisheries and Food to the Cocoa, Chocolate and Confectionery Alliance, but it lay outside their terms of reference. MAFF had found noone who saw sweet cigarettes as a serious encouragement to adult smoking but identified the main manufacturer as Barratt & Company. Officials tried to drop the idea but Newton proposed a personal approach to the chairman of Barratts and Powell agreed. Doubtingly, Dame Enid Russell-Smith asked Newton if he would be prepared to sign a letter: in the event Powell himself signed. Powell's letter set out the background and asked 'whether your firm would be likely to consider favourably a request to all manufacturers that, in the interest of the campaign against lung cancer, they should agree to discontinue producing sweets in these forms.'

Barratt's chairman, George Walsh replied in detail and at some length. He admitted some doubts about introducing any new sweet cigarette with the same name as a tobacco brand ('we hold the Trade Mark Registration 'Gold Flake' for Sweet Cigarettes' and it was one of their most popular lines) but rejected Powell's hypothesis, adding that 120 people worked on the product and that the machinery represented a capital investment of £50,000. Besides, 'many smaller manufacturers . . . would be completely put out of business if they could not make Sweet Cigarettes.' Powell asked for a draft for a 'very quick reply' but officials were at a loss what to say and asked his private office for permission to drop the matter.

Lord Newton, however, minuted Powell with his concern about the use of tobacco brand names and suggested asking them to drop these brand names. Powell provided his own draft reply, adding:

> The natural conclusion of the letter would be to try to get a discussion between Mr Walsh and an official. Unless, however, this is someone in sympathy with Parliamentary Secretary (L[ords]) and myself, the game will be lost before it starts.

The draft had a gap for evidence that the 'incidence of smoking at 12 and younger is considerable and increasing', which led to a flurry of minutes as officials, frustrated by the lack of surveys, let alone comparable surveys at an interval of time, tried to find any such evidence. (A few days after the letter was sent, the results of a survey of ten thousand children reached the Ministry: of 1,091 junior schoolchildren, aged up to 11, fewer than half said they had never smoked, and two-thirds of smokers and ex-smokers had started by the age of eight.)

Powell's reply made the most it could of alleged common ground and attempted again to recruit Walsh to the anti-smoking drive, ending by suggesting a meeting with Lord Newton. Four months later, prompted by Powell, Newton himself wrote to Walsh again suggesting a meeting. They had lunch on 9 July. Newton wrote thanking Walsh for listening and repeating his 'plea that your firm will not miss opportunities of influencing fashion away from cigarettes'. He sent a minute to Powell recording that the firm had agreed to stop advertising their cigarettes (which also included Bristol and Capstan brands - both current cigarette brands at the time) in children's papers and to 'come to an early decision about new trade names'. However, 'they would not get it past their shareholders' to discontinue production.

Powell wrote on the minute: 'The next step is to include a reference to this among other undesirable forms of influencing the young towards smoking when the opportunity next occurs, and to give the firm ample warning in advance of what one intends to say.' But shortly afterwards Powell stepped down as Minister of Health, declining to serve under Sir Alec Douglas-Home when he took over from Harold Macmillan as Prime Minister, and the file has no trace of any such follow-up.[13]

The main development in the second half of 1962, however, to which Lord Hailsham made a significant contribution, was the initiation of the voluntary codes of practice for the control of tobacco advertising that were to last - albeit heavily criticised by tobacco control experts - for nearly forty years.

The origins of the system lie with the Independent Television Authority, which was deeply concerned about the themes used to promote cigarettes and took the view it could not delay action that it was obliged to take under the Television Act to wait for Government or other decisions. The Director-General, Sir Robert Fraser, had a meeting with representatives of the industry on 31 May, as he reported the next day to a meeting of the Authority's Advertising Advisory Committee. He was most concerned about advertising that

> went beyond the direct advertising of the merits of the product itself and beyond the placing of the brand in a natural social context, to concentrate on a particular emotion or aspiration of young people. It also seemed undesirable to exaggerate the satisfaction or bliss to be derived from smoking.

He listed five types of advertising that were undesirable - and his wording includes many phrases that found a permanent place in the Cigarette Code which lay at the core of the subsequent voluntary agreements:

(1) Advertisements that greatly over-emphasised the pleasure to be obtained from cigarettes. . .

(2) Advertisements featuring the conventional heroes of the young - parachutists, racing motorists and so on - who smoked cigarettes and could be thought to inspire emulation.

(3) Advertisements appealing to pride or general manliness, i.e. 'a man's choice' or 'the cigarette for a real smoker'.

(4)   Advertisements using a fashionable social setting to support the impression that it is 'modern' and 'go-ahead' to smoke cigarettes and that smoking is part of the pleasure and excitement of 'modern living'.

(5)   Advertisements that strikingly present romantic situations and young people in love, in such a way as to link the pleasures of such situations with the pleasures of smoking.

The manufacturers had (Sir Robert reported) 'recognised the need to move with the political situation created by the [Royal College of Physicians'] Report' and had cited their elimination of advertising before 9 pm.

The Advertising Advisory Committee agreed that a code on the lines proposed was necessary and that the 'difficult question of interpretation' should be settled between the Authority and the programme companies. It received a delegation from the industry - John Partridge of Imperial, Ronald Plumley of Carreras and E J Foord of Gallaher[14] - who accepted the code in principle and agreed to replace the offending advertisements as soon as possible. They were told that it was not proposed to announce the details of the code, but the Postmaster-General would be asked to make a statement on 'very brief and general lines' in Parliament.[15]

On 17 June, more than two weeks later, Partridge was still defending advertising with a 'romantic' theme when he led a delegation of six industry representatives to meet Cary's committee of officials. He said it appealed strongly to the middle-aged and elderly, but claimed that the 9 pm threshold would lead to an overall reduction in spending (even though two days earlier he had called on MacMahon at the Board of Trade to warn him that, whereas Imperial Tobacco and Gallaher had reduced their total television advertising after the threshold decision, Carreras had made no reduction and might even be increasing it, which might force Imperial to reconsider its policy[16]). However, he made clear that the companies were finding their situation difficult: 'It was not at all certain that they could maintain silence in the face of the continued attack - Mr Partridge spoke moderately, but it was clear that he felt a strong sense of injustice . . .'[17]

On 20 June, the ITA chairman, Ivone Kirkpatrick, wrote to the Postmaster General, Reginald Bevins, describing the new Television Code, over which the manufacturers were being 'very cooperative'. It had been leaked in a report that day in *The Times*, and while it would not be published 'because of the difficulty of interpretation' they were acknowledging that the newspaper report was 'fairly near the mark'.[18]

The Ministerial Committee considered on 24 July how to deal with the manufacturers at a meeting Lord Hailsham had arranged for 31 July. The paper prepared by the officials' committee said: 'It might be suggested to the manufacturers that the course taken by the campaign, and future Government action, will turn to some extent on the policy adopted by the manufacturers in their own advertisements.' Ministers might ask if the Government could assume that manufacturers would apply the television Code of Practice to advertising in other media. 'It is unlikely that they would feel able to resist a suggestion put in this way.' The manufacturers would want to see the Code policed: the Advertising Standards Authority 'which has been set up within the last few days to police the British Code of Advertising Practice' would be a suitable body. This was disputed by the Board of Trade: a brief for the meeting which criticised the Television Code ("'Code' seems an unnecessarily dignified description to apply to this vague and woolly collection of criteria') also doubted the suitability of the Advertising Standards Authority and suggested instead a sub-committee of the Tobacco Advisory Committee![19]

The Ministerial Committee agreed that the ASA was not necessarily the 'best body to secure uniform interpretation and application of the television code in other media. The Authority had only just been set up and might not be capable of discharging so controversial a duty before it had time to establish its authority.' Moreover, Ministers were sceptical of the objectives of the Code: 'Changes in the content of cigarette advertisements would probably make no significant contribution toward the discouragement of smoking, but they might help to avert pressure for more drastic action which would be unwelcome both to the Government and to the manufacturers.'[20]

Hailsham met the Tobacco Advisory Committee on 31 July. He was accompanied by Bernard Braine, Parliamentary Secretary at the Ministry of Health, by T Fife Clark from the Central Office of Information and by his own private secretary. Facing him were Sir Alexander Maxwell, the TAC chairman, R S W Clarke and E J Partridge, chairman and vice-chairman of Imperial Tobacco, R W S Plumley and C A C Bulpitt, managing director and assistant managing director of Carreras, E J Foord from Gallaher, Geoffrey Todd as Director of the TMSC and (a new arrival) A D McCormick of British American Tobacco.

Hailsham said he hoped that an informal discussion would prove useful. The Government accepted the Royal College of Physicians' report, but, as believers in personal freedom, they would find it embarrassing to take compulsory measures. It was not the Government's purpose 'to induce any catastrophic change in smoking habits' but there would be general criticism of both Government and industry if nothing were done. The Government welcomed the voluntary restrictions agreed for television advertising and he now invited the industry 'to consider voluntarily imposing similar restrictions in the type of advertising for other advertising media'. The Ministry of Health would be conducting a long-term health education campaign, but they did not wish to be pressed into coercive measures or an advertising campaign in competition with the industry: such moves were, however, always possible.

The industry representatives said that 'on the whole they thought they would be prepared to apply to advertising generally the same sort of code which was being applied on television'. There were questions of how such a code would be adjudicated, which they would consider. Lord Hailsham said that the Government would not intend to make any announcement themselves about such an extension of the Code unless pressed and then only in the most general terms.

Maxwell wrote the next day to confirm the industry's agreement in principle:

> the interpretation of these principles and their application to the other media are not without difficulty. They will, however, give further thought to these matters - in particular to the problem of how to ensure reasonable uniformity of interpretation - and will let you know their conclusions. They will also consider whether or not it would seem desirable for the industry to announce its intentions in this regard at some suitable time.

It was not until November that the industry produced a statement: Partridge called at the Central Office of Information on 8 November to give Fife Clark a copy and, on Fife Clark's advice, Maxwell wrote the next day to Lord Hailsham, saying that since their meeting

> the tobacco manufacturers have had discussions with the Code of Advertising Practice Committee, which is, of course, responsible to the Advertising Standards Authority. As a result, the C.A.P. Committee has agreed to assist the manufacturers by making their intentions concerning advertising copy known to the Copy Committee of the various advertising media, and by generally acting in an advisory capacity to the manufacturers should it be necessary . . .

Hailsham replied welcoming the arrangements, adding: 'I should like to feel that the informal way in which we have discussed this matter is well suited to dealing with other problems of mutual interest if occasion demands.'

This may have seemed satisfactory, but the at the same time the amount of advertising was rising sharply. The subject had been raised by Bernard Braine at the meeting on 31 July: he had been told firmly that any agreement to limit advertising would fall foul of the Restrictive Trade Practices Courts and would discriminate against the smaller companies. In December a minute on the Board of Trade file records:

> Expenditure on T.V. advertising of tobacco products has risen from £2.40m. in the second half of 1961 to £2.98m. in the first six months of this year. Expenditure on Press Advertising, in the same period

shows an even more dramatic rise from £1.35m. to £2.23m., an increase of 70 per cent. Practically the whole of this increase is in respect of cigarettes (up 75 per cent) and cigars (up 104 per cent).[21]

Notes

1. PRO file BT 258.201

2. Cary of the Cabinet Office wrote to the Home Office reporting that 'the Lord President with support from his colleagues, suggested that in dealing with the question of licences to retail tobacconists . . . officials had not displayed their usual resource and ingenuity . . .' The Economic Secretary to the Treasury had reported that 'the whole system of Excise Licences for tobacco was under review and that they might be abolished [see page 81]; in this event the [Ministerial] Committee thought that the appropriate penalty under Section 7 of the 1933 Act might be a straight prohibition to sell tobacco. . .' - PRO file MH 55.2234. It was held that it was inappropriate to withdraw excise licences as a penalty for breach of the law as these were intended only for raising revenue.

3. Paper C(62)110 on CAB 129.110 and minutes CC 46(62) item 2 on CAB 128.36.

4. PRO file BT 258.201

5. Cary suggested that Powell could make the statement in the Commons, Hailsham himself in the Lords - PRO file CAB 124.1673.

6. PRO file BT 258.201

7. Monthly Bulletin of the Ministry of Health and Public Health Laboratory Service, 1963; 22: 110 - PRO files MH 55.2236, BT 258.202.

8. The Board of Trade continued to resist continued efforts by the Ministry of Health to involve them in policing advertising and promotion practices by the industry, for example by referring public complaints to them. Their absence from dealings with the industry was noted by Imperial Tobacco, who felt deserted by their sponsor department: a file note on 13 November records:

> The President [of the Board of Trade] saw Mr Clarke of Imps. during a political luncheon at Bristol last Friday . . . Mr Clarke said that he was a little disturbed to find that his dealings on smoking and health were always with the Ministry of Health or Lord Hailsham. The Board of Trade were the industry's sponsors and he would have wished the relationship to be more in evidence on this difficult problem.

Miss Boyes minuted the reason in plain terms:

> we have not felt that any useful purpose would be served by
> our forming a part of the audience at meetings which Lord
> Hailsham has held to lecture the manufacturers on their
> wickedness in purveying poison . . .

and Frederick Erroll wrote to Clarke on 10 December:

> I write now on a personal basis to assure you that we fully
> appreciate your point of view on this . . . [but as we have
> nothing useful to contribute on scientific questions we] have
> not felt that we ought to play a leading part in any publicity
> campaign on the question of health education. But I should
> like to assure you that both I and my officials are fully
> conscious of the Board of Trade's responsibility as Production
> Department for your industry and that the Board have played,
> and are playing, a full part in inter-Departmental discussions
> on questions arising out of the Report by the Royal College of
> Physicians. I should like to add that I hope the industry will
> always feel free to approach the Board of Trade . . .

- PRO file BT 258.201.

9.   A progress report circulated in January 1964 featured a report that the
     Ministry of Health stand at the Boys and Girls Exhibition at Olympia had
     featured 'diseased and healthy lungs' and 'puppets' - PRO files BT 258.201,
     BT 258.202.

10.   PRO files BT 258.1405, BT 258.201

11.   PRO file CAB 124.1672

12.   PRO file MH 82.208

13.   PRO file MH 154.174

14.   A brief prepared by the Board of Trade for a meeting with the companies by
      Douglas Jay, the President of the Board of Trade in the 1964 Labour
      Government, includes short pen pictures of Partridge, Plumley and Foord:
      'Mr E J Partridge is the newly appointed Chairman of Imperial . . . whose
      service he entered at the age of 14 some 40-odd years ago. He is able,
      ruthless, and well informed about the Board [of Trade]'s past concern with
      tobacco . . . It cannot be assumed with certainty that he will strictly preserve
      confidence on any matter touching his firm's interests.' E J Foord was 'a
      quiet, sensible man whose opinions are usually worth notice'. Of Plumley, it
      said: 'A few years ago he worked rather hard at self-advertisement, but has
      lately been quieter and reasonably helpful.' - PRO file BT 258.1406.

15.   PRO file MH 55.2234

16.   PRO files BT 258.201, BT 258.1405

17.   Paper GEN 763/14 on PRO file CAB 130.185

18.   PRO file BT 258.201

19.   PRO file BT 258:1405

20.   Paper SH(62)6 and minutes SH(62)4th, on PRO file CAB 134.2158

21.   PRO files BT 258.201, CAB 124.167

6

1963-64:
The Start of Modern
Tobacco Control

The end of 1962 can be seen as marking the start of modern policy-making on smoking and health: resistance to intervention was on the retreat and considerations and arguments still current today were elaborated, often for the first time. The proliferation of paper, as numerous avenues for possible action were explored, means that only an abbreviated treatment is appropriate here, and that biassed towards the residual official resistance to action, the personal contributions of Ministers and the rearguard actions of the industry. This means passing over comparatively lightly the solid exploration of practical policy which predominates on the files.

At the end of 1962 Lord Hailsham reaffirmed his personal interest in the subject: Cary in the Cabinet Office had enquired whether the committee of officials should continue to report to him as chairman of the Cabinet committee, still theoretically in existence, so that Hailsham 'would continue to be the Government spokesman in this matter', or should instead report through departmental Ministers. Lord Hailsham wrote:

> I am, I think, the senior non-smoker in the Cab. The more power you can get for me and for Mr Powell in this matter the better the Govt. will come out of it in the end. H. of M. *[i.e., Hailsham of Marylebone]*[1]

At this time the Ministry of Health became concerned about various methods of sales promotion for cigarettes. A paper to the Committee of Officials at the end of November expressed concern that free packs of Piccadilly cigarettes had been posted to senior civil servants and perhaps others, and that free packs of Ardath cigarettes had been put through front doors in Stevenage. 'Advertisements for Wembley cigarettes, publicising free stamps for Cope's football pools, are being pressed on all members of the public, including young children, outside stations in some parts of London'. Most particularly, the Ministry was concerned about 'coupon' promotion of brands - i.e., offering free goods from a catalogue in exchange for points or coupons collected from cigarette packs - by both Imperial and Gallaher. The paper cited the Embassy scheme's promise of 100 free points if 650 were produced by 30 April 1963 - which would require smoking almost 20 a day - and alleged that literature for the Kensitas gift scheme was being posted to girls in a secondary modern school in North London.[2]

The Board of Trade were scathing in their internal comments on this paper and put out a detailed paper on coupon schemes, tracing their history to the 1920s and quoting a 1932 Board of Trade committee that had decided they were 'not harmful to the public interest'. They reported that Carreras, which had no coupon brand, felt under some commercial pressure to introduce one but would prefer Government discouragement of such schemes on the grounds that they stimulated consumption rather than brand competition. The Board of Trade disagreed, seeing them as a legitimate trading method unlikely to proliferate as they had in the 1930s.

However, when the officials' committee met on 11 January 1963 they recommended to Lord Hailsham that coupon trading was a matter of concern calling for a fresh meeting with the industry.[3] (The Board of Trade formally dissociated themselves from this recommendation: the discussion appears to have been vigorous and led Cary to write to Miss Boyes: 'If I may say so, I do not think that at Friday's meeting you left us in any doubt about the Board of Trade view; you were admirably clear in exposition. The difficulty was rather that some of us were unable to agree with it!'[4])

In the event separate meetings were held in May and June with each of the three main companies, in which each defended its own patch and regretted the tactics of its competitors.[5] Cary recommended to Lord Hailsham that they 'let matters run for the time being', and he agreed, but stipulated that the manufacturers

> be told informally of the view (which I hold) of the imprudence from their own point of view of embarking in the present atmosphere on any method of sales promotion which justly or unjustly excites adverse comment. It could only lead to renewed public agitation for

restriction of advertising which the Government no less than manufacturers would wish to avoid.'

Attempts were later made to induce the manufacturers to agree with each other a voluntary restriction on advertising expenditure (it was first established that there would be no objection to such an agreement under the Restrictive Trade Practices Act), but these failed as the companies jockeyed for advantage.[6]

Meantime, if Carreras felt under pressure from its bigger rivals' coupon brands, they in turn were worried about its expanding advertising programme. Early in February Miss Boyes at the Board of Trade had a telephone call from Imperial's Partridge seeking a meeting with the President of the Board of Trade, Frederick Erroll, for his chairman, R W Clarke, and Mr Mason, the chairman of Gallahers. 'What appears to be worrying the two firms is the pressure which they feel upon them to maintain and possibly extend their advertising as a result of Carreras' drive and the fear that this may be thought to be inconsistent with the Government's attitude on smoking and health.'

In preparation for that meeting, the two companies provided extensive briefing which showed that spending on tobacco advertising had risen from £9 mn. in 1961 to £11 mn. in 1962 and that within the total Carreras' share had leapt from 14% to 21%, even though its market share was under 5%. The two big companies (Imperial had 59% and Gallaher, expanding rapidly, 36%) had tried to negotiate with Carreras a limit on spending on television and press advertising, both in total and in particular on coupon brands, but the talks had collapsed. Erroll was briefed for the meeting with a summary of the Government's actions ('Both the Minister of Health and the Lord President would have liked to go a good deal further than this and are disposed to take a fairly forceful line in public statements'):

> All this leaves the manufacturers in what is now an extremely competitive business in an invidious position. They are very conscious of their public face and do not wish their advertising to appear to be operating in opposition to Government policy. On the other hand the Monopolies Commission has told them [in a recent report] that they must be competitive and in any case the aggressive growth of Carreras is forcing them to be so. The bigger companies might be excused for feeling that a ban on advertising would have certain advantages; it would almost certainly strengthen their hold on the market.

The brief hastened to rule out any such ban on advertising and to warn that even if the companies could agree a limit it might fall foul of the regulations on restrictive practices.

When Erroll met the two companies on 22 February, they set out their concerns and he urged them to 'be statesmanlike for a further year to see how the pattern developed', pointing out that 'the opponents of smoking could mount a most damaging case: cigarette advertisements and cancer deaths had both increased in 1962 and this showed the lack of response by the industry to a major national problem'.[7]

At the Ministry of Health Bernard Braine, the Parliamentary Secretary, received a deputation from the Advertising Inquiry Council. This was a voluntary pressure group, involving Charles Fletcher and other doctors, Francis Noel-Baker MP and representatives of the churches, teachers and others. (Selby-Boothroyd wrote a minute describing them as 'a small band of self-appointed reformers anxious to carry on the unfinished work of the late Oliver Cromwell'.) The Council had produced a report condemning tobacco advertising in April 1962 and now they drew attention to the growth of advertising and of coupon brands and the recovery of cigarette sales against a background of ineffective Government action. They called for control of advertising, including a ban on television advertising, and a full-scale publicity campaign.

> Dr Fletcher said that it was his conviction, based on talking with his patients, that the public disregarded mere exhortation from the government. The public would not believe that the government was serious in its campaign until it took effective action . . .

> The Parliamentary Secretary [Bernard Braine] said that he must reject any suggestion that the Ministry was not serious in its campaign. This was, however, a task of persuasion, not compulsion . . . Over 1 million posters had been distributed, appropriate film rights had been acquired and films had also been produced or were in preparation; the mobile education vans were fully booked and the establishment of anti-smoking clinics was encouraged. [8]

The campaign was indeed beginning to lose some of its amateurish nature. The Central Office of Information tested new poster designs in focus group discussions ('Yes I smoke but then I'm just another sheep . . .' won little support, and a coffin labelled 'Flip-top box for Smokers' was thought 'too far-fetched, ridiculous and untrue') and they wrote a 50-page report after similar testing of the film *Smoking and You* (recording that smokers were far more difficult to convince than non-smokers).[9] New posters were sent out to the press - in November 1963, two, called 'Father and Son' and 'Mother and Daughter', carried the caption: 'Think before you smoke: Are you setting a good example?' A three-month £12,000 campaign was launched in January 1964 in twelve weekly and three monthly boys' and girls' magazines with advertisements featuring 'Bobby Moore - professional footballer (England and West Ham) . . . Jim Clark - world Motor Racing Champion . . . Diane Clifton Peach - Olympic Ice Skating Champion . . .the President of the Cambridge University Boat Club . . . ' (Oxford had not yet replied). Short 'filmlets' were prepared for showing on BBC television.[10]

The Ministry sent a circular to Regional Hospital Boards on smoking in hospitals ('particularly inappropriate . . . the general attitude . . . should . . .be one of discouragement. On the other hand, a complete ban will not usually be practicable at present').[11] The Health Education Coordinating Committee was told in October 1963 that at the Ministry's request non-smoking accommodation on two London Underground lines had been experimentally extended to two-thirds of the carriages. The campaign budget was increasing, £10,000 was budgeted in 1963/64 for a public opinion survey, and in January 1964 a 39-page report was circulated. (Thirty-eight percent of adults wished to quit smoking, 14% already had; one in three current smokers thought their health was being affected; two in every three adults thought smoking should be banned in theatres and cinemas and large minorities supported bans in restaurants, buses and offices. Between 24% and 33% even of adult smokers favoured banning advertising in various media. The commentary, however, found little encouragement in these figures.) Another survey was carried out at a cost of £15,000 in May/June 1964.[12] The BBC television soap opera *Compact*, set in the offices of a women's magazine, had a storyline about a feature on stopping smoking; a National Savings poster depicting young people smoking was withdrawn and the Ministry of Health passed on complaints to the BBC about excessive smoking in *Z-Cars*.

Even so, attitudes were still unsure and equivocal. When a press officer, L W Jefferies, suggested to Dodds, the Ministry of Health undersecretary, that 'increased Government sponsored advertising on T.V. should not necessarily be ruled out because of the fear of massive retaliation by the tobacco firms. The message we want to put over is a strong one and is difficult to counter or to swamp . . .' the thought was novel enough for Dodds to annotate it: 'A very interesting expression of views which we should keep with our pps. [papers] on advertising.' The Treasury complained that the Ministry of Health was breaking the rules by not charging for the hire of its films on smoking and health (but later backed down). Heald wrote from the Ministry to Buckinghamshire's Medical Officer of Health about a proposed postal franking slogan 'Cigarettes can Kill' to which the post office was objecting: 'I cannot help feeling that it goes a bit far and cannot fail to be open to strong criticism (not wholly unjustifiable) that it represents undue exaggeration and is, therefore, in breach of the principles of the code of advertising practice. For this reason, and because we feel that it is unwise psychologically and practically to overstate our case, I very much regret that I cannot support your case with the G.P.O. and their agents . . .'[13]

The Ministry of Education reported that teachers were 'discouraged in their efforts to press home government propaganda against smoking' by 'the lack hitherto of positive action by the government vis-à-vis advertising, especially T.V. advertising' and in the Health Education Coordinating Committee there was continued criticism of the inadequacy of the campaign:

the representatives of the BMA and the Association of Municipal Corporations claimed that 'many people and local authorities regarded the Government's ambivalent attitude to television advertising as proving that they were only half-hearted about the subject.'[14]

The degree of ambivalence in that attitude was made fully apparent when the BMA representative on the ITA's Advertising Advisory Committee moved a total ban on tobacco advertising. The Committee comprised four members each from advertising, from public life and from the medical world, including the Ministry of Health. Its advice was for the time being mandatory on the ITA (this was due to change shortly when the Television Act 1963 came into force). On 29 January 1964 the Postmaster General, Reginald Bevins, wrote to Anthony Barber, who had replaced Enoch Powell as Minister of Health, seeking that the Ministry's representative on the Committee should not vote for a television advertising ban:

> Whatever the merits of a ban itself, I must confess that such action by a Ministry of Health official cannot fail to be construed as a direct result of a Government decision that cigarette advertising on television should be banned. It seems to me that your representative should continue to abstain. . . The feeling [at the Cabinet on 12 July 1962] was that if the Government is seen to exercise influence in one field of advertising then the whole question of compulsory control of advertising generally cannot fail to come into question.

Barber wrote: 'Could Mr Dodds be considering a short statement for our representative to make which would set out the Govt's position (as decided by Cabinet), but without his voting in favour of the ban. I think that the P.M.G. has a cogent argument here.' However, he seems to have been persuaded otherwise: the same day, he received a minute from the deputy secretary A W France referring to a proposal by Quintin Hogg (as Lord Hailsham had now become) to reconvene his Cabinet committee on smoking:

> The Secretary (who is now away till tomorrow) was opposed to the revival of the L.P.'s committee. But I do not think it will be possible to stop it, especially as we are now in some dispute with the Post Office about the action to be taken. That being so, I think we should use the L.P.'s committee to settle our line in the ITA's Advertising Advisory Committee.

and later that day he wrote to Hogg. Government policy had hitherto, he wrote, been not to 'pick out television from the other advertising media and apply a ban on it' but this was now a new situation and 'it might seem odd for the Ministry of Health representative to fail to support a move that is designated to further this [government publicity] campaign'.

The Ministerial Committee met on 5 February. In discussion, it was said that if the Ministry of Health representative voted for a ban, it would imply that the Postmaster General should enforce a ban even if the Advisory Committee voted against it and would imply that the Government should 'seek powers to stop cigarette advertising in other media'. But it would be odd for a Ministry of Health representative on an independent body not to support such a proposal. 'To do so could, if known, be represented as indicating that the Government were not ready to accept the implications of their declared view that smoking was a danger to health.' It was decided that the Ministry of Health should abstain but should not argue against the ban, rather quoting the Government decision not to single out television, and should 'strongly attack' any suggestion that the connection between smoking and lung cancer was not established.

In the event the Committee rejected the proposal for a ban, deciding merely to prohibit advertisements 'suggesting that it was better from a health point of view to smoke one brand of cigarette rather than another'.[15]

The Ministerial Committee had been revived in order to consider the first report from the US Surgeon General on smoking and health, published in January 1964.[16] This was a detailed scientific survey of all the research, by contrast with the Royal College of Physicians' report, which was written for the general public. The subordinate committee of officials met on 29 January, being told by their chairman, Cary, according to Selby-Boothroyd's report on the Board of Trade file, that

> this new burst of interest was prompted by Mr Hogg (who was described as 'having the bit between his teeth'), following the publication of the U.S. report . . . It was suggested by the chairman that once a start was made on banning advertising it would be a 'slippery slope' which could end only in a total ban on all forms of sales promotion - with nationalisation of the industry as the only way of doing it . . .

> The Ministry of Health (Mr Dodds) suggested that all cigarette packets might be made to carry a warning, such as 'cigarettes cause lung cancer', but this seemed too much for the rest of the Committee . . .

> It is very clear that there is a firm conviction that the manufacturers can be 'directed' under the shadow of their fear that legislation will otherwise be introduced. So long as this attitude (which I do not admire) continues, I think it is important that we should attend these meetings.

The Committee, whose initial view was that the US report did not advance in principle beyond the Royal College of Physicians' report two years earlier, despite its greater detail, prepared over the next few months a detailed paper for the Ministerial Committee on the American report and its possible implications.

In their report, issued in mid-June, they noted that the US report had led to the US industry adopting a much more detailed code of advertising practice than the British one and to the Federal Trade Commission requiring mandatory health warnings on all cigarette packs and advertisements. The committee of officials was attracted by the potential effectiveness of packet warnings but troubled by the principle of requiring manufacturers to discourage the use of their own products. The officials saw no advantage in the American advertising code but were concerned at the growth of tobacco advertising and rehearsed the arguments for and against a ban on television advertising without reaching any recommendation. They reported that smokers of coupon brands smoked more heavily than others - but that the manufacturers had suggested that such brands attracted heavy smokers rather than stimulating heavy smoking.

They recommended requests not to smoke in post offices, employment exchanges and other Government offices open to the public but opposed legislation to impose a ban. They opposed differential taxation of cigarettes as against cigars and pipe tobacco but seem not to have considered a straightforward increase in taxation all round, although their arguments about the effects on poor smokers and on the cost of living index show that they were unlikely to have welcomed the idea. They still opposed any large-scale advertising campaign in the mass media in competition with tobacco advertising ('even £1 million per year . . . would still be much less than the advertisers spend, but yet far more public money than the Government could, we suggest, properly spend') but they proposed that some paid advertising on public transport and at stations would help reach 'the mass of the adult working population' with whom little contact had yet been made.

This was the only positive recommendation in the report. Dodds, the Ministry of Health undersecretary, will have been disappointed: in a minute he had written to the deputy secretary A W France that this extension of the publicity campaign was one of the department's main objects, but

> I would myself put the banning of cigarette advertising on television right at the top of the priorities as the measure most likely to impress on the public and on those who are working with us in the health education campaign that the Government really believes that cigarettes are a serious danger to health and is in earnest in its efforts to reduce this danger. I would put the warning on cigarette packets second and non-smoking notices in Government offices a poor third.[17]

He got none of the three.

In the Board of Trade Selby-Boothroyd was relieved: sending the report to his new undersecretary, M M Ord Johnstone, he wrote: 'It is an honest report, even if the M. of Health may be disappointed, and it does not recommend any plunge into legislation.' Johnstone replied complacently: 'I agree with you that the report is a commendably honest document - the kind of thing, in fact, which shews the Civil Service at its rare best.'[18]

The Ministerial Committee considered the officials' report on 30 June. Noting public criticism of the limited nature of their interventions, they speculated that 'people, while continuing to smoke as before, were now more anxious about the effects of smoking and more likely to criticise the Government for not taking effective steps to reduce smoking; but it did not follow that any such measures would necessarily be more welcome to public opinion than previously'. Thus bolstering their unwillingness to take action, they agreed to the limited advertising campaign recommended, deferred until after the impending General Election consideration of warnings on packets, and decided against any further steps on any other front. Quintin Hogg, doubtless disappointed, was asked to report their conclusions to the Prime Minister.[19]

Four months later there was a change of Government. On 30 October one of his staff sent J P Dodds at the Ministry of Health a press cutting quoting Harold Wilson, the new Prime Minister, as having said before the election: 'The advertisements for cigarettes should certainly now be stopped - certainly on television - and I don't see why we shouldn't ask all the newspaper proprietors to cut them out in newspapers.' Dodds prepared a draft letter for his Minister to send to colleagues suggesting a meeting to clarify the new Government's policy.[20]

Notes

1.	PRO file CAB 124.1674

2.	The Board of Trade found itself obliged to take on the role of bringing apparent abuses to the companies' attention. Selby-Boothroyd, while mocking the whole idea, took inordinate pride in having won an apology in August 1963 from Gallaher when the father of a 17-year-old girl complained about 1,000 cigarettes being offered as a prize in a 'twist' (dancing) competition: he was still boasting of it in a brief written in January 1964 - PRO file BT 258.202.

3.	Papers GEN 763/16, GEN 763/17, GEN 763/18 and minutes GEN 763/6th, on PRO file CAB 130.185

4.	PRO file BT 258.201

5.	The meetings are reported in papers GEN 763/22-25, of which GEN 763/24 is a summary on coupon trading for the Lord President. - PRO file CAB

130.185.

6.   PRO file CAB 124.1672

7.   PRO file BT 258.201. The Board of Trade's attitude towards the industry at official level is further illustrated in November 1963 when the Ministry of Health sought more detailed figures for tobacco sales than were then available. A C Young, Industries and Manufactures Department Division 3, passed the request to Imperial Tobacco but added: 'Although the present letter can be taken as passing on to you a request made by the Ministry we are not attempting to persuade you in any way to comply with it . . . We would have no reluctance in telling the Ministry of Health that they could not have this new set of figures if that is what the industry decides. We are content for you to apply only the criterion of the industry's interest . . .' - PRO file BT 258.202.

8.   PRO file BT 258.202

9.   PRO file MH 151.26

10. PRO files BT 258.202, BT 258.203

11. PRO file MH 154.182

12. PRO file MH 151.26

13. PRO file MH 154.182. The Medical Officer of Health in Buckinghamshire was George Townsend, 'one of the best in Britain and a leader of his group' (Sir George Godber, personal communication, 19 January 1998).

14. PRO file BT 258.203

15. PRO files MH 154.182, CAB 130.185, CAB 134.2158

16. Sir George Godber recalls: 'When the RCP report came out I bought 10 copies and sent them to my counterparts in the US, Canada, Australia, New Zealand, the four Scandinavian countries, Holland and France. Luther Terry (U.S. [surgeon-general]) was so impressed by the report that he set up his own committee which led to this report and continuing activity. Canada, NZ, Norway and Sweden did the like.' (Personal communication, 19 January 1998)

17. PRO file MH 151.29

18. PRO files BT 258.202, BT 258.203, CAB 130.185

19. PRO file CAB 134.2158

20. PRO file MH 154.182

Epilogue

The record speaks for itself.[1] Fourteen years after Hill and Doll were 'satisfied that the case against smoking as such is proven'[2], ten years after the publication of the first report on their study of British doctors, seven years after the Medical Research Council told the Government that 'the evidence now available is stronger than that which, in comparable matters, is commonly taken as the basis for definite action' and two years after the Royal College of Physicians in exasperation produced a popular summary of the evidence with specific policy recommendations, the Government was still equivocal about taking effective action against this egregious cause of disease and premature death.

Of course, one must make allowances. 'The past is a foreign country: they do things differently there.' Government was still relatively small. It was less ready to intervene in people's everyday lives. The tobacco industry was of enormously greater importance to the Treasury than it is now. Only part of the damage done by smoking had yet been recognised: its contribution to heart disease, in particular, was still only tentatively identified. The addictive power of tobacco had not yet been recognised, so that there was on the one hand greater willingness to leave to individuals the 'free' decision whether to continue smoking and on the other the fear that high-profile action to discourage smoking might precipitate a wholesale collapse in the market with serious economic implications. Few economists realised how resistant to price increases demand would be.

Nevertheless, the precedents and evidence were there for those with eyes to see. Government did conduct mass health campaigns directed at combatting diphtheria or promoting immunisation. Ministers and civil servants did not have to cow-tow to the potentates of the industry to the extent they did. In 1956 Robin Turton as Minister of Health was already telling the Cabinet that deaths from lung cancer had risen from 1,880 in 1931 to over

17,000 in 1955. Lennox Johnston back in the 1930s had even described smoking as an addiction and guessed that nicotine was the active ingredient. Enoch Powell noted the 'probable flatness of the demand curve'.

But the prevailing ethic was one of doing the bare minimum to protect the Government from criticism for doing nothing while avoiding creating any effect for which one might have to answer. Among officials a few - notably Sir George Godber - struggled to overcome the inertia[3] but too many - especially outside the Ministry of Health - sought only to reflect or encourage their Ministerial masters' lack of enthusiasm. Among Ministers, indeed, throughout the whole period only Enoch Powell and Lord Hailsham treated the problem with the seriousness and application it deserved - and they were frustrated by colleagues unwilling to disturb the even tenor of their ostrich ways.

In 1964, NOP surveys showed that 67% of men and 36% of women still smoked, and that, when asked whether smoking was a cause of cancer, only one in three smokers answered Yes.[4]

Notes

1.   For another (similar) assessment, which I have discovered as this book goes to press, see Webster C: *Tobacco Smoking Addiction: A Challenge to the National Health Service*, British Journal of Addiction 1984; **79**: 7-16.

2.   Sir Harold Himsworth's words - see page 12 above.

3.   Sir George's reports as Chief Medical Officer from 1960 were notably outspoken and a later article in *The Times* said that 'Sir George Godber has embarrassed the Government about as much as a civil servant can'. Sir George himself comments that Sir Bruce Fraser, Arnold France (shortly to succeed Fraser as Permanent Secretary), James Dodds and 'one or two others . . . went as far as they could against the obstruction of other departments.' He adds in further mitigation that 'the RCP report was the first good presentation of the case at a time when its full strength still wasn't known, and the American follow-up two years later gave a huge boost.' (Personal communication, 19 January 1998)

4.   40% of all adults answered No, 17% answered that they did not know, and 43% (only 34% of smokers) answered Yes. The two surveys were in September and July 1964 respectively - PRO file MH 151.26.

Appendix

Official statements

1:   12 February 1954:
Iain Macleod, Minister of Health: Written Answer

The Standing Advisory Committee on Cancer and Radiotherapy have had this matter under consideration for three years.   As a result of preliminary investigations, a panel under the chairmanship of the Government Actuary was set up in 1953 to inquire and report.   I have now been advised by the Committee in the following terms:

> Having considered the report of the panel under the chairmanship of the Government Actuary on the statistical evidence of an association between smoking and cancer of the lung, and having reviewed the other evidence available to them, the Committee are of opinion: -
>
> (1)   It must be regarded as established that there is a relationship between smoking and cancer of the lung.
>
> (2)   Though there is a strong presumption that the relationship is causal, there is evidence that the relationship is not a simple one, since:-
>
> > (a)   the evidence in support of the presence in tobacco smoke of a carcinogenic agent causing cancer of the lung is not yet certain;
> >
> > (b)   the statistical evidence indicates that it is unlikely that the increase in the incidence of cancer of the lung is due entirely to increases in smoking;
> >
> > (c)   the difference in incidence between urban and rural areas and between different towns, suggests that other factors may be operating, e.g., atmospheric pollution, occupational risks.
>
> (3) Although no immediate dramatic fall in death-rates could be expected if smoking ceased, since the development of lung cancer may be the result of factors operating over many years, and although no reliable quantitative estimates can be made of the effect of smoking on the incidence of cancer of the lung, it is desirable that young people should be warned of the risks apparently attendant on excessive smoking.   It would appear that the risk increases with the amount smoked, particularly of cigarettes.

I accept the Committee's view that the statistical evidence points to smoking as a factor in lung cancer, but I would draw attention to the fact that there is so far no firm evidence of the way in which smoking may cause lung cancer or of the extent to which it does so.   Research into the causes of lung cancer has been pressed forward by the Government and by other agencies in view of the increase in the incidence of this disease and we must look to the results of its vigorous pursuit to determine future action.

I should also tell the House that before these recommendations were considered by Her Majesty's Government the tobacco companies had offered to give £250,000 for research. They have, on my advice, agreed to offer this money to the Medical Research Council.

2: 12 February 1954: Ministry of Health: Press statement

The Parliamentary Answer given <by> the Minister of Health today (Friday) (of which a copy is attached) is based on advice given to him by his Standing Advisory Committee on Cancer and Radiotherapy who for three years have been giving close consideration to the problem of the possible relationship between tobacco smoking and cancer of the lung. In view of the public interest and concern over this question it is, in the Minister's opinion, of very great importance that uninformed and alarmist conclusions should not be drawn from the Committee's advice and that the qualifications mentioned by the Committee in their advice should be fully realised.

In the Autumn of 1950 an article by Dr. Doll and Professor Bradford Hill in the *British Medical Journal* suggested that, on evidence arising from a statistical enquiry, there was a relationship between smoking and cancer of the lung. The Committee at that time considered that further evidence was needed. Late in 1952 a further article by Dr. Doll and Professor Bradford Hill, which confirmed their earlier conclusions, reports from research workers in the U.S.A., and the submission of arguments seeking to demonstrate that the relationship was not proved, led to a panel under the Chairmanship of the Government Actuary being asked in 1953 to enquire and report to the Standing Advisory Committee. The conclusions reached by this panel were considered by the Standing Advisory Committee who advised the Minister as in the attached statement.

Although it can be taken as established that a relationship between smoking and lung cancer exists, it is important to realise that this relationship is not a simple matter, that a great deal of information and research is still required and it is not possible to draw final conclusions. The Minister considers that it would be helpful, in order that the matter can be looked at in proper perspective, to set down firstly what facts are known about the relationship, and secondly what must be regarded as speculative and unproved.

Facts Which Are Known

The Minister would like to draw attention to the following facts, which are now well established:-

(1)   There has been an increase in deaths from lung cancer in this country which began about 1919 and has continued ever since. The increase is much greater in males than females. Between 1911 and 1919 the number of deaths from cancer of the lung was about 250 per year. The rise which began about 1919 can be illustrated from the figures of deaths for 1931 as compared with subsequent years. In 1931 the number of deaths attributed to lung cancer in England and Wales was 1,358 for males and 522 for females. Those figures represented 5% of all *cancer* deaths and 0.5% of deaths from all causes in males, and 2% of all *cancer* deaths and 0.2% of deaths from all causes in females. The latest figures available, for 1952, showed a further increase in that 11,981 males and 2,237 females died from the disease. These represent 26% of all *cancer* deaths and nearly 5% of deaths from all causes in males, and 5% of all *cancer* deaths and 1% of deaths from all causes in females. The figures also show that the highest mortality rate from lung cancer in males occurred in the 65-74 age group, whereas in females the highest rate occurred in the 75 and over age group.

(2)   Comparable increases have been reported in all countries from which reliable statistics are available. Factors such as the increasing age of the population and better diagnosis account for some of the rise but not the whole of it.

(3)   Tobacco smoking lays some part in this increase. To use the language of statisticians, there is an "association".

(4)   It is certain that tobacco smoking cannot be the only factor since the disease occurs in non-smokers. Not one but several factors or a combination of factors must be regarded as responsible.

(5)   The disease is more prevalent in urban areas than rural and different parts of the country suffer more than others.

(6)   No substance producing cancer of the lung has yet been specifically identified in tobacco smoke. Certain tars derived from tobacco smoke have produced skin cancers in mice but this is not considered as being conclusive evidence of the presence of a substance producing cancer of the lung.

So much is known.

Further Evidence Needed

The following matters must, however, remain speculative until further evidence comes to light:-

(i)   There is no firm evidence of the way in which smoking may cause lung cancer or of the extent to which it does so. All that can be said at present is that there is a presupposition that it does, but the evidence does not permit us to say any more than that.

(ii)   The difference in incidence between town and country and between different towns suggests that other factors should be taken into account such as atmospheric pollution or risks from particular occupations, but no evidence is available of the extent to which these factors operate.

(iii)   Although the risk of contracting the disease appears to increase with the amount smoked, particularly of cigarettes, no reliable factual estimate can be made of the precise effect of smoking.

In view of this, it is not possible to come to a final and definite conclusion on this matter. A good deal of research and information is needed before anything more firm can be said. Many investigations are taking place both in this country and abroad which bear directly on the problem and also into the related problem of the effect of atmospheric pollution on health. The Ministry are in close touch with the Medical Research Council on this, and there will be no hesitation in launching further research if any particular line shows promise. Opportunity is taken of paying tribute to the valuable pioneer work of Dr. Doll and Professor Bradford Hill and other workers who have given us what little information we have.

3:   7 May 1956:
Robin Turton, Minister of Health: Oral Answer

Since my predecessor made a statement in February, 1954, investigations into the possible connection of smoking and cancer of the lung have been proceeding in this and other countries. Two known cancer-producing agents have been identified in tobacco smoke, but whether they have a direct role in producing lung cancer, and if so what, has not been proved.

The extent of the problem should be neither minimised nor exaggerated. The number of deaths from cancer of the lung has risen from 2,286 in 1931 to 17,271 last year. To place the figures in perspective - in 1954, out of every thousand deaths of men aged between 45 and 74, 77 were from bronchitis, 112 were from strokes and apoplexies and 234 were from cancer, of which 85 were cancer of the lung. Deaths of women from cancer of the lung are still not very significant and represent a small fraction of the total.

The chairman of a committee of the Medical Research Council which has been investigating the subject considers that the fact that a causal agent has not yet been recognised should not be allowed to obscure the fact that there is, statistically, an incontrovertible association between cigarette smoking and the incidence of lung cancer. The statistical evidence from this and other countries to which he refers tends to show that mortality from cancer of the lung is twenty times greater amongst heavy smokers than amongst non-smokers.

The Government will take such steps as are necessary to ensure that the public are kept informed of all the relevant information as and when it becomes available.

In answer to supplementary questions, Mr Turton said:

In my view, in the present stage of our knowledge, a national publicity campaign would not be appropriate.

It would appear that pipe smokers face a heavier risk than non-smokers, but the risk is substantially less than that incurred by heavy cigarette smokers. . . . [T]here is some evidence that the risk of contracting cancer of the lung decreases when smoking is given up.

Whenever any more knowledge becomes available, I shall deem it my duty to put it before the House at once. . . . I did tell the House some time ago that two cancer-producing substances had been identified in tobacco smoke.

4:   27 June 1957:
Statement by Minister of Health

In their Annual Report, and more particularly in their special report on tobacco smoking and cancer of the lung . . . the Medical Research Council have advised the Government that the most reasonable interpretation of the very great increase in deaths from lung cancer in males during the past twenty-five years is that a major part of it is caused by smoking tobacco, particularly heavy cigarette smoking. The Council point to the evidence derived from investigations in many countries in support of this conclusion, in particular to identification of several carcinogenic substances in tobacco smoke.

2.   The Government feel that it is right to ensure that this latest authoritative opinion is brought effectively to public notice, so that everyone may know the risks involved in smoking. The Government consider that these facts should be made known to all those with responsibility for health education. The Minister of Education included in his recently published Handbook for Teachers on Health Education advice about the dangers of smoking and he is circulating copies of this statement to local education authorities and education authorities generally. Corresponding action will be taken by the Scottish Education Department in Scotland. The Government now propose to bring these views to the notice of local health authorities who are concerned under statute in the prevention of illness and who are responsible for health education as a means of prevention. Local health authorities will be asked to take appropriate steps to inform the general public and in this task they will have the assistance of the Central and Scottish Councils for Health Education.

3.   Once the risks are known everyone who smokes will have to measure them and make up his or her own mind, and must be relied upon as a responsible person to act as seems best.

4.   The Medical Research Council are at present supporting an extensive programme of work designed to discover the way in which tobacco smoke exerts its effect and the relative importance of other factors, such as atmospheric pollution, which may also play a part in the causation of lung cancer. The recent expansion of this programme has been greatly assisted by a substantial grant made in 1954 by a leading group of tobacco manufacturers; on the advice of my predecessor, the present Minister of Labour, this sum was given to the Medical Research Council with complete discretion as to the choice of research projects to be supported and to the publication of results.

5.   The work at present in progress consists largely of chemical and biological studies of the many different constituents of tobacco smoke and atmospheric pollution. In addition, surveys of the role of atmospheric pollution and of specific industrial hazards in the causation of the disease are being undertaken. Work along these lines is being supported in many centres in different parts so the country and the Council have also established as part of their own organisation three new research groups in Exeter, London and Sheffield, where long-term studies of different aspects of the problem are being carried out. Every opportunity will be taken by the Medical Research Council to pursue any promising new lines of research which may become apparent.

5:   27 June 1957:
Medical Research Council statement:
'Tobacco Smoking and Cancer of the Lung'

The Increase in Lung Cancer

In their Annual Report for 1948-50 the Council drew attention to the very great increase that had taken place in the death rate from lung cancer over the previous twenty-five years. Since that time, the death rate has continued to rise, and in 1955 it reached a level more than double that recorded only ten years earlier (388 deaths per million of the population in 1955 compared with 188 in 1945). Among males the disease is now responsible for approximately 1 in 18 of all deaths. Although the death rate for females is still comparatively low, it also has shown a considerable increase in recent years and the disease is now responsible for 1 in 103 of all female deaths.

Three comments may be made on these figures. In the first place, the trend over the last few years indicates that the incidence has not yet reached its peak. Secondly, the figures are not to be explained as a mere reflection of the introduction and increasing use of improved methods of diagnosis but must be accepted as representing, in the main, a real rise in the incidence of the disease, to an extent which has occurred with no other form of cancer. Thirdly, only a small part of the rise can be attributed to the larger numbers of older persons now living in the population; in the last ten years the lung cancer death rates among both men and women have risen at all ages from early middle-life onwards.

Possible Causes of the Increase

The extent and rapidity of the increase in lung cancer point clearly to some potent environmental influence which has become prevalent in the past half-century and to which different countries, and presumably also men as compared with women, have been unequally exposed. The pattern of incidence of the disease rules out any possibility that the increase can be due, in a substantial degree, to special conditions, such as occupational hazards, affecting only limited groups. It is necessary to seek some factor or factors distributed generally throughout the population, and in considering the possibilities it must be borne in mind that a very long period, 20 years or more, may elapse between exposure to a carcinogenic agent and the production of a tumour. From the nature of the disease attention has focussed on two main environmental factors : (1) the smoking of tobacco, and (2) atmospheric pollution - whether from homes, factories, or the internal combustion engine.

Smoking as a Cause of Lung Cancer

(a) Epidemiological Surveys

The evidence that heavy and prolonged smoking of tobacco, particularly in the form of cigarettes, is associated with an increased risk of lung cancer is not based on the observation that the substantial increase in the national mortality followed an increase in the national consumption of cigarettes. It is derived from two types of special inquiry. In the first, patients with lung cancer have been interviewed and their previous histories in relation to smoking and other factors that might be relevant have been compared with those similarly obtained from patients without lung cancer. The results of nineteen such inquiries (in this country, the U.S.A., Finland, Germany, Holland, Norway and Switzerland) have been published. They agree in showing more smokers and fewer non-smokers among the patients with lung cancer, and a steadily rising mortality as the amount of smoking increases. In the second type of inquiry, information has been obtained about the smoking habits of each member of a defined group in the population and the causes of the deaths occurring *subsequently* in the group have been ascertained. There have been two such investigations, one in the U.S.A. covering 190,000 men aged 50-69, and the other in this country covering over 40,000 men and women whose names appeared on the Medical Register of 1951. In both, the results have been essentially the same. The investigation in this country, which has now been in progress for more than five years, has shown with regard to lung cancer in men

(1)   a higher mortality in smokers than in non-smokers;

(2)   a higher mortality in heavy smokers than in light smokers;

(3)   a higher mortality in cigarette smokers than in pipe smokers;

(4)   a higher mortality in those who continued to smoke than in those who gave it up.

It follows that the highest mortalities were found among men who were continuing to smoke cigarettes, heavy smokers in this group having a death rate nearly 40 times the rate among non-smokers. Although no precise calculation can be made of the proportion of life-long heavy cigarette smokers who will die of lung cancer, the evidence suggests that, at current death rates, it is likely to be of the order of 1 in 8, whereas the corresponding figure for non-smokers would be of the order of 1 in 300. The observation on the effect of giving up smoking is particularly important, since it indicates that men who cease to smoke, even in their early forties, may reduce their likelihood of developing the disease by at least one half.

It should be noted that the excess of deaths from lung cancer among smokers was not compensated for by any corresponding reduction in the number of deaths from cancer of other sites in the body; in other words, there was a total incidence of cancer in the smoking groups in excess of the incidence that would have prevailed in the absence of smoking.

It will be apparent from what has been said that the evidence from the many inquiries in the last eight years, both in this country and abroad, has been uniformly in one direction and is now very considerable. It has been further strengthened recently by the observation from several sources that the extent of the relationship with smoking differs for different types of lung tumour which can be distinguished only by microscopic examination.

Laboratory Evidence

From the physical and chemical point of view there is nothing inherently improbable in a connection between smoking and lung cancer. Tobacco smoke consists largely of microscopic oily droplets held in suspension in air, and these droplets are of a suitable size to be taken into the lungs and retained there. Over a hundred constituents have so far been identified and, among these, five substances have already been found which are known to be capable, in certain circumstances, of causing cancer in animals. Some workers have succeeded in producing tumours in animals by painting concentrated extracts of tobacco tar on the skin. Known carcinogens are present in tobacco smoke in very small amounts however, and there is no certainty that such low concentrations could be harmful to human beings. Nevertheless, the finding of carcinogenic agents in tobacco smoke is an important step forward, in that it provides a rational basis for the hypothesis of causation.

Atmospheric Pollution as a Cause of Lung Cancer

It has been known for some years that mortality from lung cancer is greater in urban areas than in the countryside. This fact, together with the identification of carcinogenic substances in coal smoke and in motor vehicle exhausts, has led to the supposition that exposure to atmospheric pollution may be concerned with the increase in lung cancer. The role of atmospheric pollution is particularly difficult to investigate however, and the evidence is neither so consistent nor so extensive as that relating to tobacco smoking. On the one hand, no excess mortality from lung cancer has been observed in persons who would be especially exposed by the nature of their work to atmospheric pollution, for example transport workers, garage hands and policemen. On the other hand, the results of a number of investigations have suggested that a relationship does exist between atmospheric pollution and lung cancer. Perhaps the best evidence for this relationship comes from studies of the small number of deaths from the disease among *non-smokers* in different types of residential district; in these studies higher death rates have been observed among non-smokers in large towns than among those in rural areas. On balance it seems likely that atmospheric pollution plays some part in causing the disease, but a relatively minor one in comparison with cigarette smoking.

Assessment of the Evidence Relating to Smoking and Lung Cancer

Knowledge of the causation of lung cancer is still incomplete. Many factors other than tobacco smoking are undoubtedly capable of producing the disease; for example, at least five industrial causes have been recognised. Nevertheless, the evidence for an association between lung cancer and tobacco smoking has been steadily mounting throughout the past 8 years and it is significant that, during the whole of this period, the most critical examination has failed to invalidate the main conclusions drawn from it. It has indeed been suggested that the fundamental cause may be some common factor underlying both the tendency to tobacco smoking and to the development of lung cancer some 25 to 50 years later, but no evidence has been produced in support of this hypothesis.

In scientific work, as in the practical affairs of everyday life, conclusions have often to be founded on the most reasonable and probable explanation of the observed facts and, so far, no adequate explanation for the large increase in the incidence of lung cancer has been advanced save that cigarette smoking is indeed the principal factor in the causation of the disease. The epidemiological evidence is now extensive and very detailed, and it follows a classical pattern upon which many advances in preventive medicine have been made in the past. It is clearly impossible to add to the evidence by means of an experiment in man. The Council are, however, supporting a substantial amount of laboratory research which may throw more light on the mechanism by which tobacco smoke and other suspected causative factors exert their effect, and which may thus eventually add to the degree of proof already attained as a result of studies of human populations. It must be emphasised, however, that negative results from work with animals cannot invalidate conclusions drawn from observations on man.

Conclusions

1. A very great increase has occurred during the past 25 years in the death rate from lung cancer in Great Britain and other countries.

2. A relatively small number of the total cases can be attributed to specific industrial hazards.

3.   A proportion of cases, the exact extent of which cannot yet be defined, may be due to atmospheric pollution.

4.   Evidence from many investigations in different countries indicates that a major part of the increase is associated with tobacco smoking, particularly in the form of cigarettes.   In the opinion of the Council, the most reasonable interpretation of this evidence is that the relationship is one of direct cause and effect.

5.   The identification of several carcinogenic substances in tobacco smoke provides a rational basis for such a causal relationship.

6:   12 March 1962:
Enoch Powell, Minister of Health: Oral Answer

My right hon. Friend the Secretary of State for Scotland and I are asking local health authorities to use all their channels of health education to make the conclusions of the [Royal College of Physicians'] report widely known and to make clear to the public the dangers to health of smoking, particularly of cigarettes. We shall be giving them guidance and providing them with publicity material. We are also consulting with the Central and Scottish Councils for Health Education about ways in which they can help. As regards health education in the schools, my right hon. Friend the Minister of Education is answering a Question today.

In answer to supplementary questions, Mr Powell said:

There is no direct comparability between the sum spent by local health authorities and the sums spent on advertising.

[T]his report is undoubtedly an extremely valuable and powerful weapon in the hands of health education which the Government will now be actively supporting. The other suggestions made in the report of the Royal College are under consideration by the Government.

I shall be providing local health authorities with free publicity material, and I shall be in consultation with them and with the Central Council for Health Education as to the most effective form which that material might take. I have under consideration the suggestion of anti-smoking clinics which is made in the Royal College's report. I have in mind that experiments might be made in that direction.

The Government certainly accept that the report demonstrates authoritatively and crushingly the causal connection between smoking and lung cancer and the more general hazards to health of smoking.

The question of television advertising, as of advertising generally, is dealt with in the suggestions made in the report which, as I have said, are under consideration by the Government. I have no doubt, however, that, apart from the steps to be taken by my right hon. Friend the Minister of Education, the health education work of local health authorities will have young people very much in mind. Health education work is undoubtedly one of the most effective channels for getting this message over in the right places, and I shall certainly give it every support I can.

Index